his or her family. For professionals, *The Obsessive-Compulsive Trap* will provide much-needed insight into this often debilitating illness.

Glen Havens, M.D.

The absence of clearly written and clinically relevant material on OCD has contributed to poor recognition and treatment of this problem. I applaud Dr. Crawford's book as a major contribution for helping patients and clinicians understand OCD better. I have a list of patients who are waiting to read *The Obsessive-Compulsive Trap*.

Michael R. Lyles, M.D.
PSYCHIATRIST
BOARD MEMBER, THE AMERICAN ASSOCIATION OF CHRISTIAN COUNSELORS

Dr. Mark Crawford has done an outstanding job of revealing the truth about obsessive-compulsive disorder. He has explained what is going on emotionally, spiritually, genetically and biochemically. He has done a great job of showing how OCD can be successfully treated and how people who are diagnosed with this disorder can live very normal lives with either therapy or medication or both. As a psychiatrist who has treated hundreds of patients with OCD, I highly recommend *The Obsessive-Compulsive Trap* and definitely plan to ask my OCD patients and their loved ones to read this book so that they will understand that OCD is a very treatable disorder.

Paul Meier, M.D.
AUTHOR, *BRUISED AND BROKEN: UNDERSTANDING PSYCHOLOGICAL PROBLEMS* AND *HAPPINESS IS A CHOICE*
FOUNDER, MEIER CLINICS
WWW.MEIERCLINICS.COM

The Obsessive-Compulsive Trap

Real Help for a Real Disorder

MARK E. CRAWFORD, PH.D.

Regal

From Gospel Light
Ventura, California, U.S.A.

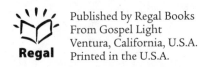

Published by Regal Books
From Gospel Light
Ventura, California, U.S.A.
Printed in the U.S.A.

Regal Books is a ministry of Gospel Light, a Christian publisher dedicated to serving the local church. We believe God's vision for Gospel Light is to provide church leaders with biblical, user-friendly materials that will help them evangelize, disciple and minister to children, youth and families.

It is our prayer that this Regal book will help you discover biblical truth for your own life and help you meet the needs of others. May God richly bless you.

For a free catalog of resources from Regal Books/Gospel Light, please call your Christian supplier or contact us at 1-800-4-GOSPEL *or* www.regalbooks.com.

Cover design by David Griffing

Library of Congress Cataloging-in-Publication Data

Crawford, Mark.
  The obsessive-compulsive trap / Mark Crawford.
    p. cm.
Includes bibliographical references.
  ISBN 0-8307-3489-9
  1. Obsessive-compulsive disorder. I. Title.
  RC533.C735 2004
  616.85'227—dc22   2003026317

1 2 3 4 5 6 7 8 9 10 11 12 13 14 15 / 10 09 08 07 06 05 04

Rights for publishing this book in other languages are contracted by Gospel Light Worldwide, the international nonprofit ministry of Gospel Light. Gospel Light Worldwide also provides publishing and technical assistance to international publishers dedicated to producing Sunday School and Vacation Bible School curricula and books in the languages of the world. For additional information, visit www.gospellightworldwide.org; write to Gospel Light Worldwide, P.O. Box 3875, Ventura, CA 93006; or send an e-mail to info@gospellightworldwide.org.

Acknowledgments

I would like to thank my wife, Dana, for her continued support in this endeavor. Her encouragement and confidence in my ability to finish this project were invaluable to me. I would also like to thank my parents for encouraging me early in my life to seek God's will for my life and to "pursue whatever He is calling you to do."

No colleague has been more helpful and influential to my career than my friend and partner, Michael Lyles, M.D. I want to acknowledge his significant contribution to Chapter 8 on medication. Thanks, Michael, for being like a brother to me, and for your influence and help throughout my career. I want to thank my patients who have honored me by allowing me to help them with their lives and families, and who have taught me more than they realize. Finally, I want to thank God for the privilege of being able to help others in this area; but mostly for inviting me into an intimate relationship with him through the gift of salvation in Jesus Christ.

Contents

Introduction

While most people have heard of Obsessive-Compulsive Disorder (OCD), few people really understand it. In the movie, *As Good As It Gets,* Jack Nicholson portrayed a man who suffers from OCD. Audiences laughed as Nicholson's character washed his hands compulsively, stepped over cracks in the sidewalk, and used his own cutlery in a restaurant to avoid possible germs. The television show *Monk* showcases a brilliant but quirky investigator who suffers from OCD. In fact, his illness is one of the main themes of the show. Recently, I've heard many people jokingly comment on a friend's fastidious behavior by calling them "Monk." However, to individuals suffering from OCD, the symptoms are no laughing matter.

It is estimated that 1 in 40 people in the United States suffer from OCD. Many of these individuals suffer in relative silence and are unaware that this is a very treatable condition. Because of the nature of the symptoms, OCD also affects people closely associated with the person suffering from the disorder. Consider the following facts about OCD:

1. OCD is a biological condition that results primarily from a deficiency in the neurotransmitter serotonin in the brain.
2. OCD tends to run in families. Therefore, people probably have a genetic predisposition toward the disorder.
3. According to the Obsessive-Compulsive Disorder Foundation,

approximately 1 in 40 people in the United States are diagnosed with OCD. As many as twice that number may have suffered from OCD at some point in their lifetime.

4. OCD can begin in childhood and often manifests in children of preschool age.

5. The average person sees 3-4 doctors and spends over 9 years seeking treatment before receiving a correct diagnosis.

6. Some studies have found that it takes an average of 17 years from the time OCD begins for people to obtain appropriate treatment.

7. With proper diagnosis and treatment, most people who suffer with OCD can find significant relief from the disorder.

8. It is believed that many famous historical figures probably showed significant symptoms of OCD (e.g., John Bunyan, Winston Churchill, and Martin Luther).

If you or someone you know suffers from OCD, this book was written for you. This book is designed for patients and families affected by OCD as a resource that can be read relatively quickly. It is hoped that after reading this book, the reader will have a good understanding of what OCD is and what OCD is not. It is also my desire to educate the reader about the very effective treatments that are available for OCD.

The first two chapters of this book explain the two basic symptoms of OCD: obsessions and compulsions. Chapter 3 discusses the biological causes of the disorder. Chapter 4 describes how OCD manifests in children and teenagers. OCD in children is often overlooked or misdiagnosed as attention or behavior problems. Chapter 5 is designed to clarify the confusion that many Christians have about the symptoms of OCD and spiritual issues. Chapter 6 discusses disorders associated with OCD (Obsessive-compulsive spectrum disorders and co-morbid disorders). Chapters 7 and 8 discuss treatment options. Finally, Chapter 9 describes some actual cases from my practice to illustrate how OCD manifests and is treated. My hope is that this book will help the reader understand OCD and realize that help is available in order to alleviate the tremendous suffering this disorder causes for millions of people.

ONE

Obsessions

Obsessive-compulsive disorder is characterized by two main categories of symptoms: obsessive thoughts and compulsive behaviors. The terms obsessive and obsession are used in everyday conversation to suggest a preoccupation. For example, a person may be described as being obsessed with money. The term obsession is frequently used to describe a passion or strong interest. For example, "Golf is Howard's current obsession." However, in discussing OCD, the term obsession is used differently. Obsessions refer to intense thoughts, worries, or images that are experienced as intrusive and unwanted. These obsessions cause great anxiety for an individual and often lead to the development of compulsive behaviors or rituals designed to decrease anxiety. I'll discuss compulsive behaviors more in Chapter 2. One of the simplest ways to describe an obsession is an unrealistic or overexaggerated worry or concern about something. The person experiencing an obsessive worry will frequently describe a thought or concern that sounds magnified or "catastrophized" to others. In other words, they will talk about a fear or worry that is far beyond what most people consider "normal." In fact a person with OCD can sometimes tell you that they realize that their fears or worries are irrational or illogical. However, the anxiety is very real and overpowering. I've talked with many patients who tell me that they know their worries are irrational; however, they can't control the overwhelming fear and anxiety that these obsessive thoughts produce. Obsessions usually fall into one of several categories.

Contamination Obsessions

These types of obsessions frequently involve excessive concern over germs, diseases, and other contaminants.

Tammy was a young girl who was fourteen years old when her parents brought her to me. Her parents indicated that they felt Tammy "worried too much." Worry is a common presenting problem for people who suffer from OCD. Tammy's worries included fears that something may happen to her parents; fears that something may happen to her sister; and worry about germs. Tammy was so concerned about germs; she was unable to use any restroom outside of her home. Traveling was terrifying for her. Even family vacations that were designed to be fun and stress free became a source of tremendous anxiety and stress for Tammy and her family. If the family had to stay in hotels, Tammy would make sure that she brought several cans of Lysol spray with which she would immediately "disinfect" the entire hotel room upon arrival. This would enable her to feel "safe" enough to at least be able to use the restroom. At home, Tammy simply could not use any public restroom. If she went out with friends to a movie, she made sure that she would use the restroom just before leaving. During an outing with friends, she was always careful not to drink too much liquid so she would not have to urinate. She timed her outings to make sure that she would never be out longer than she could wait to use the "safe" restroom of her own home. The biggest challenge she faced was from Monday through Friday at school. While Tammy did use the restroom before leaving home and restricted her fluid intake, she could not make it through the entire school day before she had to yield to the call of nature. Since she could not use the school restroom, she would actually leave school and return home to use the bathroom. Needless to say, Tammy missed most of her afternoon classes. In fact, she missed so many of these classes she actually failed two of them.

While people who suffer from OCD often have a general fear of germs, some people with OCD have specific fears related to a particular disease. For example, many people with OCD report a specific fear of contracting AIDS. Most of the time, these individuals are not in any "high risk" group for contracting HIV (the virus that leads to the development of AIDS). However, their fear and anxiety is extraordinary. This fear often causes them to ruminate endlessly that they may be HIV positive. They are not comforted by reassurance that there is no reason to believe they should be concerned (e.g., no unprotected sexual encounters; no blood transfusions; etc.). They begin to describe irrational fears such as believing that they might have had an undetected cut on their skin (the hand, for example) and they wonder if they may have shaken hands with someone who was infected with HIV thus resulting in the transmission of the disease. This example illustrates the type of thought processes characteristic of obsessive thinking. Probabilities are greatly exaggerated and logic is stretched to arrive at the ultimate conclusions. Many of these people will have multiple medical tests to make sure that they aren't infected. However, a negative test may lead to further rumination and obsession. They may begin to wonder, "What if the test was wrong; after all, they aren't 100 percent accurate. Perhaps I should be retested." Some OCD patients will receive repeated tests for a disease that they are at virtually zero risk of contracting. Others will do the opposite: they are so terrified that they may have the disease they will refuse to receive a test to assuage their fears. They reason, "If I am HIV positive and find out, I won't be able to carry on. It's better to not know." While HIV isn't the only specific disease OCD sufferers worry about, it is a common one.

Another frequent obsessive worry is that of getting cancer. Jeff was a young man who read an article about testicular cancer and became terrified that he would develop this disease. Consequently, he worried almost incessantly about having the disease. This was a bright young man who functioned at a very high level. He was at the top of his graduate school class in his studies, and everyone found him fun to be around. However, he was almost constantly tormented by obsessive thoughts that he had testicular cancer. He described experiencing "sensations" in his scrotum. He read that while the disease is often symptom free in the initial stages, there may be a "heavy feeling" in that area. He began to imagine that he felt a "heaviness" in this area which further fueled his anxiety and concern. At times, obsessions can involve an imagined physical sensation. These are known as somatic obsessions. The only time he was not assaulted by these thoughts and fears was when he was mentally engaged in a task, or when he was distracted by something he thoroughly enjoyed. He found that he was almost anxiety free when he drank alcohol.

Consequently, he began to drink more. OCD can be a precipitant to abuse of substances. Many OCD patients described using alcohol, marijuana, or other drugs to "self-medicate," or to decrease the anxiety caused by the obsessive thoughts.

People who suffer from OCD are particularly at risk of developing obsessive worries that they may have a disease after reading about the symptoms of a particular disease. Some OCD sufferers will see a television show or read an article about an obscure disease or illness and begin to worry that they may have the symptoms of that malady.

For some people with OCD, the obsessive worry is not of contracting a specific disease, but rather a pervasive fear of any germs that they may come in contact with. This may become so extreme that they fear touching doorknobs (because myriad other people have touched them) or handling money. Their persistent worry about germs causes anxiety in almost any public arena. Efforts to avoid being "contaminated" with germs can lead to the development of significant compulsive behaviors (discussed in Chapter 2).

While some individuals obsess about contracting an illness, others may obsess about contaminating others. These concerns range from mild (a man who worries excessively that he will spread germs if he coughs in public) to more severe (a woman who fears that her past sexual indiscretion may have caused her to contract a sexually transmitted disease that she will pass on to innocent others by simply rubbing against them).

Some individuals worry about being contaminated not by germs, but by other "contaminants." Many individuals report a fear of being harmed by ordinary household cleaners. Bobby was a teenage boy who was terrified of household cleaners. When his mother would spray the kitchen counters with a normal household product, he would experience severe anxiety (bordering on a panic attack). He avoided all cabinets and rooms where cleaning supplies were stored.

Other individuals report anxiety over the possibility of environmental contaminants. These may include chemicals such as pollutants and pesticides. Some individuals refuse to allow their homes to be sprayed for pests or their lawns to be sprayed for weeds for fear of being harmed by the toxins used in these types of treatments.

The Need for Symmetry or Exactness

Many people with OCD describe the need for things to be "evened up." This refers to the need for things to be symmetrical. For example, some people go to great extremes to make sure things in their environment are even on each side. They may arrange their rooms or offices so that things are aligned in perfect symmetry including pictures on walls, items on their desks, or books on a shelf. These individuals may also report the need for things to be symmetrical on their body. I've spoken with several individuals who described tying and retying their shoes in order to make sure they were tied with the exact same tension on each foot. I worked with a young man who had to make sure that if he saw something out of the corner of one eye, he also viewed it with the other eye. This became quite cumbersome as he worked to make sure that things were always "even." While these behaviors would be considered compulsive (which we will discuss in detail in the next chapter), it is the obsessive need for symmetry that drives the behavior.

A similar type of obsessive thought is the need for exactness. This refers to a need for certain things to be "just right." A middle-school student was failing in classes involving a great deal of writing. This was perplexing to her parents and teachers since she was such a bright and capable student. She was originally referred to me in order to see if she suffered from some biologically based attention problems (such as attention-deficit hyperactivity disorder) or some type of specific learning disability (such as written expression). I performed a complete neuropsychological evaluation in order to examine all areas of cognitive functioning. Testing revealed a young woman who was highly intelligent with achievement scores to match her intellect (indicating no areas of learning disability). She also manifested no obvious signs of attention difficulties, and teacher and parent reports indicated no significant difficulties in these areas. However, in completing the testing, I observed that she took an inordinate amount of time to complete written tasks. An analysis of her performance determined that she was obsessed with forming letters on the page perfectly. Her handwriting was impeccable and letters looked as though they were formed by a printer rather than a human. She made frequent erasures in her efforts to make the letters perfect. This need to make her written work perfect caused her to take at least 5 times longer in completing work. This was causing her to miss handing in assignments at school because she could not complete them in time. Homework became so arduous; she would become frustrated and quit. This case is an example of how students who suffer from OCD are often suspected of suffering from other disorders such as attention-deficit hyperactivity disorder (ADHD) and learning disabilities.

For others, the need for exactness involves positioning things in their environment. One young woman I worked with described spending hours making sure the fringe of her oriental rug was "perfectly straight on all sides." She also described becoming very anxious if a guest moved one of the pillows on her couch from its "perfect position." I had one patient who told me she could not concentrate on our session until she straightened every diploma and picture on my walls and lined up the items on my coffee table so they were precisely positioned.

Aggressive Obsessions

Many OCD sufferers are tormented by intrusive fears that they may suddenly and violently act on angry or violent impulses. Typically, these individuals have no history of violence or trouble with aggressive behavior. However, they are terrified that they may suddenly engage in some violent act as though it is outside of their control. I worked with a woman who became panic stricken around babies. When I asked her why she was so anxious around infants, she described with great difficulty the fear that she may suddenly rip the child from the parents' arms and slam the child to the ground. This woman was a highly skilled and very successful paraprofessional. She had no history of any aggressive or violent behavior in her 40+ years of life. In fact, she loved children and was deeply saddened that she could not be around her nieces and nephews because of this paralyzing fear. Her anxiety was completely irrational, and she knew this. However, she was disturbed that these thoughts were even in her conscious mind. She described how she was haunted by images of seeing herself being handed an infant. She talked about how she would see herself raise the small baby above her head and throw it to the ground with all her might. She then talked about how she was traumatized by seeing the image of the child lying on the ground, bleeding and dead from the blow. These images were so gruesome and clear, so terrifying and traumatic, that they were debilitating to her. She was so horrified by these thoughts that she went to great lengths to avoid having them. Unfortunately, this primarily meant avoiding her sister, nieces, and nephews.

I've spoken to several individuals who experienced significant anxiety around knives. In fact, I've known a few individuals who had to remove all knives from their house (which made cooking difficult). If these individuals saw a knife, they were bombarded by horrific images of taking the knife and sticking it into their eye. Again, none of these individuals had any history of self-harm. However, these horrific images and the fear of their possible aggressive impulses were terrifying.

For others, these obsessions take the form of violent images alone as opposed to fears of violent impulses. I spoke with a teenager who described riding by a house on his way to school when he observed a man mowing his yard. The teen was blindsided by a sudden image of the man falling under the lawnmower and having his leg severed by the mowing blade. This image was extremely upsetting to the young man. After this, the teen was unable to ride by the same house (because of the anxiety this image created for him) and asked his mother to take him to school via a different and less convenient route.

Many others live with agonizing thoughts and fears of

something terrible happening to loved ones. They may have images or fears of loved ones dying in motor vehicle accidents or plane crashes. Others may experience extreme anxiety caused by thoughts of loved ones being attacked and assaulted.

For many, these fears of something terrible happening to loved ones is accompanied by the belief that if they do something (e.g., recite a certain prayer or engage in a certain ritual), they can protect the loved ones from harm. The feeling of responsibility for protecting their loved ones is overwhelming and can cause great distress.

Religious Obsessions

Because I frequently work with Christians, I see obsessions involving religion frequently. One of the most common religious obsessions is the fear that the person has "committed the unpardonable sin." Others describe the fear that they have "blasphemed the Holy Ghost." When asked what they think they may have done to warrant eternal condemnation, the answers vary. However, they are convinced that they may have done something to deserve eternal separation from God. Because of the confusion in the Christian community over this and other religious obsessions and compulsions, I've devoted an entire chapter to this topic (see chapter 5).

Sexual Obsessions

Some people with OCD find any type of sexual thoughts and feelings unacceptable and extremely anxiety producing. This is particularly true of adolescents suffering with OCD. Eric was a young man who experienced an episode of sexual acting out early in his pre-puberty years. The incident was handled appropriately by his parents and was in the past. However, the teen harbored extraordinary feelings of guilt and shame over the incident. He later associated any and all sexual feelings with this incident and had tremendous difficulty accepting his normal sexual development. He would become extremely distressed upon waking after having had a nocturnal emission. He also described seeing a television show in his basement which caused him to become sexually aroused. Because of his difficulty with accepting his normal sexual feelings, he began to view the T.V. and eventually the entire basement as "contaminated." By the time he came to see me, he could not go into the basement of his own home. In fact, anything that was in the basement was viewed as "contaminated" and was at risk of contaminating the remainder of the house. He would not wear his favorite clothing or listen to his favorite CD's because they were in the basement.

I recall another young man who was tormented by the fear that he would become attracted to other males. The curious fact was that he never had the slightest attraction to other males. In fact, the thought of this actually repulsed him. However, he was so preoccupied by the fear that he may someday find another man attractive, he would go to great lengths to avoid establishing any close relationships with other male friends.

While it is true that some individuals can become obsessed with sexual thoughts and feelings in an almost addictive way, the type of sexual obsessions I am referring to here are different. Sexual obsessions associated with OCD refer to extreme discomfort with *normal and healthy* sexual thoughts, feelings, and impulses.

Doubting obsessions

Some individuals with OCD find themselves constantly questioning their own behaviors. For example, they may wonder if they locked doors or turned off appliances. I worked with a man who was late for work every day. I don't mean a few minutes late, I mean *very late*. The only reason he wasn't fired from his job was because he was a terrific guy and a valued worker. The reason for his tardiness was his inability to leave the house due to his fears that he may not have unplugged the coffee pot or closed the garage door. He described returning to the kitchen repeatedly to make sure the coffee pot was unplugged. He would also stare for long periods of time in order to "make sure" it was unplugged. He reasoned that if he stood and stared long enough, he would surely remember that it was unplugged. However, after being gone for a few minutes, his doubts would return and he would have to go and check again. He also described sitting in the driveway for a prolonged period of time staring at the garage door in order to make sure it would not somehow reopen. After leaving the house, his doubts would return and he would have to return to the house in order to check again.

Hoarding Obsessions

Some people with OCD are referred to as "pack rats" because of their inability to throw anything away. These people will save any and all items (regardless of how useless they may be). They often realize that they may be running out of space to store things. However, when they are faced with the need to make a decision to throw something out, thoughts run through their mind such as, "What if I need that item some day?" These thoughts are so strong they stop the individual from being able to discard even useless items. Consequently, they begin to gather and collect piles of useless junk. Imagine the distress this causes family members.

"Just So" Obsessions

This last category of obsessions is a bit difficult to describe. However, if you suffer from OCD, you will know exactly what I am describing. Many people with OCD feel that certain things must be done in a certain way. They may have trouble explaining what that way is or why it must be done that way. However, they know that it must be done "just so." A man described one such obsession to me and demonstrated with his hands. He stated that he often had the urge to take his hands and position them so that the fingers of his left hand touched the tips of his right hand at precisely the ends of the finger. He stated, "I'm not sure how I know when they are touching at that particular spot, but it has to be exact. I know when I've done it because it feels right. Then I can stop and go on to whatever I need to do." This man was a successful executive for a Fortune 500 company. He told me that he could do this in a business meeting and no one had a clue that he was engaging in the behavior. Again, I am describing an example of a compulsive behavior. However, it is the obsessive thought of having to have it "just so" that drives the behavior.

These are examples of a few types of obsessions. Obsessions are a hallmark symptom of OCD. They are thoughts, worries, images, or impulses that torment the individual and feel out of the person's control. Typically, obsessions are irrational and illogical and may be recognized as such by the individual.

However, they cause debilitating anxiety and distress and usually result in the development of compulsive or ritual behaviors which I will discuss in the next chapter. It is important to understand obsessions so that the person can recognize when they are being plagued by obsessive thoughts or images. Identification of these obsessions is essential to proper understanding, diagnosis and treatment.

TWO

Compulsions

In the last chapter we discussed the first hallmark symptom of OCD—obsessions. The second chief characteristic of OCD is the development of compulsive behaviors. The term compulsion is another one used frequently in everyday language. Behaviors that are excessive are often described as compulsive. For example, people have been described as compulsive shoppers; compulsive eaters; or compulsive gamblers. However, when talking about OCD, the term compulsion is used differently. Compulsions are behaviors that are usually done in an attempt to decrease the anxiety caused by obsessive thoughts. These behaviors typically feel like they "must be done." Consequently, the person with OCD feels unable to control them. Usually, compulsions are done to accomplish one of the following:

1. to prevent something bad from happening
2. to "undo" the thought or feeling associated with an obsession
3. to minimize or temporarily eliminate the anxiety caused by an obsessive thought

Compulsions often must be done in a certain manner, and at times, must be repeated over and over. They can be behavioral or mental in nature and typically fall under one of the following categories.

Cleaning/Washing Compulsions

These types of compulsions are often in response to obsessive thoughts about contamination described in Chapter 1. Tammy was the girl who could not use a public restroom because of her fear of "germs." When traveling with her family, she carried several bottles of Lysol spray in order to disinfect the room in order to enable her to use the restroom in a hotel. This would be considered a compulsive behavior; she felt an overpowering need to clean the bathroom of the hotel in a manner that was far beyond what would be considered "normal" cleaning.

In Chapter 1, I mentioned the case of Eric who experienced severe anxiety over any normal sexual feelings or thoughts. His anxiety resulted from the obsessive thoughts associated with normal sexual feelings. However, his difficulties did not stop with obsessive thoughts. Eric was so uncomfortable with anything associated with his sexuality, he felt "contaminated" if he touched his genitals in any way—even while showering. In fact, whenever Eric touched his genitals, he felt the need to go through an elaborate hand-washing ritual. He explained that after he used the restroom, he would wash his hands while slowly counting to 15. Afterward, he would begin again, washing thoroughly while counting to 15. After a third round of washing and counting to 15, he felt "clean" and could stop. He even felt the need to engage in this hand-washing ritual when he touched his genitals while showering. This often resulted in extraordinarily long showers (taking up to 40 minutes). This would often cause Eric to be late for school. Because of this compulsive washing ritual, Eric would not allow himself to shower with his basketball team after practice. It was too embarrassing for him to go through this ritual in front of his teammates.

Compulsive hand washing is not an uncommon symptom among people who suffer from OCD. In fact, many people who suffer from compulsive hand washing suffer from extremely dry and chapped hands to the point of needing a topical treatment for this skin condition.

It is well known that Howard Hughes, once the wealthiest man in America, suffered from severe OCD. Howard Hughes was a successful businessman, inventor, pilot, and movie producer. In his later years, his OCD was so severe that he lived his remaining years as a secluded hermit. He was rich enough to have a staff of workers to care for him, and he gave them specific instructions on how to prepare food for him. He was known to write memos for each step of food preparation and included very specific and elaborate instructions regarding how to wash a tin can before opening it in order to eliminate the risk of germs.

The T.V. show *Monk* shows the title character's cleaning compulsions in the show's opening each week. Adrian Monk is shown sterilizing his toothbrush with boiling water from a tea kettle; he is shown vacuuming the area where the walls in his home meet the ceiling; and he is shown compulsively washing the window in his home.

Checking Compulsions

Compulsively checking things is usually in response to obsessive fears or doubts. Typically, a person with OCD will feel assaulted by a thought that something was not done, and they will feel compelled to go back and check to make sure that it is. Examples include checking to make sure doors or windows are locked and making sure appliances are turned off (e.g., stoves; coffee pots; lights; etc.). Most of the time, the checking is done to prevent something terrible from happening. For example, the person checks the locks to make sure that no one breaks in; checks the stove to make sure it doesn't stay on and start a fire; etc. It is estimated that well over half of all people with OCD engage in some type of checking compulsions.

Steve was a thirty-eight-year-old married man whom I met because I was treating his daughter for OCD. Steve was a faithful husband, devoted father, and reliable worker. In fact, I doubt you could find anyone who had anything negative to say about Steve. Unfortunately, Steve was tormented by OCD. He disclosed his personal battle with OCD as we started discussing his daughter's illness and how OCD is a genetic, biological disorder. Steve's disorder made leaving the house a daily nightmare. He described spending inordinate amounts of time staring at the coffee pot to make sure it was unplugged after breakfast. He told me, "I figured if I looked long enough, I'd be convinced that it was unplugged so I wouldn't have to go back and check it again." Steve was plagued by a checking compulsion. It was not uncommon for him to recheck to make sure the coffee pot was unplugged up to a dozen times each morning before finally being able to leave the house. His behavior was becoming irritating to his wife. She started to have little patience for his frequent checking. Unfortunately, his ordeal did not end when he left the house. His next hurdle came after he backed his car out of the garage and closed the garage door with his automatic garage door opener. He sat and stared for up to three minutes to make sure that it was "really closed." He frequently would pull out of his driveway and feel forced to turn around to go back and check and make sure the garage door was really closed. This ordeal could add up to half an hour to his morning routine. By the time he finally reached work, his checking compulsions started again as he returned to his car several times to make sure that he had actually locked the car door. Because Steve's OCD was making him late for work, he started getting ready for work several hours earlier than he needed to in order to accommodate his compulsions. This would give him time to check and re-check and still make it into work on time. Unfortunately, this resulted in sleep deprivation and an unusually long work day for him.

To people who have never suffered from OCD, they probably will not understand why Steve was not convinced after checking once. In fact, it is not uncommon, nor is it a sign of OCD to occasionally go back and check to see if something is locked or turned off. However, the need to repeatedly re-check compulsively is different. People with OCD have difficulty explaining that they "must" re-check despite the fact that they checked only moments ago. Typically, this is due to the obsessive doubt that plagues the OCD sufferer. They are not easily reassured by checking and feel the need to check and re-check over and over. For some, there is a need to check a certain number of times (usually a particular number that has special meaning to the OCD sufferer) in order to feel sufficient reassurance.

For some people with OCD, the checking is even less "rational." For example, many people with OCD are tormented by obsessive thoughts that they may have harmed someone or something. In order to alleviate the extreme worry, they must check and re-check to make sure they did not cause harm.

Alex was a ten-year-old boy who was brought to my office for help. He was a quiet and shy young man who was a good student and never got into trouble. His symptoms strongly suggested OCD and included an obsessive fear that he may have damaged his family's car or furniture in the house. This anxiety led him to go back and check the item in question to make sure it was not damaged. When asked how he thought he may have damaged the car, for instance, he stated that he had a thought that when he walked by the car, he may have accidentally brushed the car with his coat causing the zipper to scratch the paint. This would precipitate a series of trips to the car during which he would check every inch of the car to make sure that the paint was not scratched. One trip was not enough to reassure him; therefore, he made several trips and was usually only reassured when a parent went with him to make sure that everything was O.K.

Glen was a young man in his thirties who suffered from OCD. One of Glen's more painful symptoms involved the cycle that occurred when he drove in his car. If Glen drove alone, he would frequently get blindsided with the thought that he may have hit someone with his car. This was often precipitated by Glen hitting a minor bump in the road. Immediately, the thought would pop into his head that, "That may have been someone you just ran over. If you don't go back and check, they could die." Despite his efforts to resist, Glen's anxiety would build until he could no longer stand it at which point he would turn around and drive back to the spot where the thought started in order to make sure there was no unfortunate victim in the road.

Checking can take other forms as well. Recall the individuals who feared that they may be infected with the virus that causes AIDS. For many of these people, they feel the need to obtain numerous blood tests in order to confirm that they are not HIV positive (a test result indicating that they are infected with the virus that leads to AIDS). For many of these individuals, receiving news that their blood test is negative for the HIV virus offers only brief relief from their anxiety. Their obsessive thoughts return shortly afterward, and they feel the need to get re-tested. This pattern of behavior is an example of compulsive checking.

John was a successful professional who worried frequently that he may have cancer. His anxiety caused him to frequently check for irregularities on his body. For example, he spent hours looking over his skin to make sure there were no unusual moles or skin spots. At one point, he thought he felt a "lump" in his neck. He checked it so frequently that by the time he got to his doctor to ask about it, his doctor told him that there was nothing to be concerned about and all tests were negative. However, he apparently had "checked" the same area in his neck so often, he had aggravated the tissue around the area and caused some swelling and bruising.

Repeating Rituals

Some people with OCD repeat behaviors that are not necessarily directly related to a particular obsessive fear or doubt. Unlike checking compulsions in which the compulsive behavior is directly connected to the fear of the consequences of not checking, repeating compulsions can appear to be random. Examples include re-writing certain words or letters; repeating certain words or phrases; or repeating certain behaviors (such as walking in and out of a doorway or up and down a particular set of stairs).

Typically, the person describes a need to re-do the behavior for no apparent or logical reason. When pushed to explain why they must repeat the behavior, the best (and most honest) explanation they can offer is that they don't know why, but there is great anxiety that something bad may happen if they do not repeat the behavior.

Wesley is a high-school sophomore who described getting "stuck" in his home because he had to walk back and forth, in and out of a certain doorway that led from the kitchen to his room. Whenever he had to take this particular route, he always made sure that he walked through the door using his left foot first, then he backed up and repeated this 6 times— no more and no less. Since there was no other way to get from his room to the rest of the house, this was a frequent ordeal.

Lisa is a high-school junior who suffers from OCD. Her morning ritual is also arduous. She is tormented by obsessive thoughts that she may get into trouble at school. These thoughts are persistent and severe despite the fact that she has never been in trouble before. Her compulsive routine involves the need to think a certain thought (a mental compulsion) while getting dressed in the morning. If she feels that she has not thought the "right" thought while putting on an article of clothing, she will take the article off and put it back on while attempting to think the correct thought. This makes her feel that she has protected herself from getting into trouble for that day. Unfortunately, putting on clothes while thinking just the right thought is a bit more of a challenge than it sounds. Consequently, Lisa frequently spends up to 40 minutes simply getting dressed in the morning. She is rarely on time for her carpool and has no explanation for her tardiness since it would be far too embarrassing for her to try to explain her reasons for being late.

Hoarding Compulsions

Compulsive hoarding refers to an inability to discard worthless items. This is very different from an individual who collects a certain type of item (e.g., sports memorabilia; stamps; coins; etc.) for profit or entertainment. Compulsive hoarding typically involves a person being unable to throw away worn out or useless items primarily because of the fear that they may need the item later and won't have it, or that someone else will need it, and it will be gone. The fear is that they will be unable to deal with the guilt of having thrown out something that will one day be necessary. Consequently, they often accumulate piles and piles of useless junk in their homes, cars, or offices.

Beverly was a woman who saved everything. She could justify everything she kept as something that might have a particular use some day in the future. Even obviously broken items were saved with the explanation that "it could be fixed good as new." Initially, Beverly was referred to good-naturedly as simply a pack rat. However, her husband began to lose his sense of humor when Beverly's "collection" of junk began to compete with their living space. The attic and garage filled after a while. Later, Beverly's "junk" started accumulating in the guest bedroom. They could no longer accommodate guests in their home as the only spare bedroom was filled with boxes and bags of useless stuff. Her hoarding compulsion soon caused a major marital crisis that actually threatened the future of their relationship.

Ordering/Arranging Compulsions

Ordering or arranging compulsions involve lining things up in a certain order; arranging things in a certain pattern; and positioning things so that they are "just so." This is different from simply being neat and organized. These types of compulsions are often specific to certain items or certain places. I often hear parents say, "My child can't be OCD because his room is a mess." This statement reflects a misunderstanding of OCD—that all people with OCD are overly neat and organized. This is simply untrue. There are some people with OCD that have arranging and ordering compulsions that may make them appear to be overly neat and organized. However, there are many people with OCD who do not have this symptom and who are fairly unorganized.

The type of ordering and arranging associated with this compulsion goes well beyond what would be considered functional or adaptive to the individual. One could easily argue that it is good to be neat and organized. However, with this type of compulsion, the motivation is not to be organized and more efficient, but to order and arrange things in a particular fashion because to *not* do it that way causes great anxiety and discomfort.

A few years ago, the movie *Sleeping with the Enemy* portrayed an abusive husband who had to have the towels hanging at exactly the same length. He also insisted on having the labels on the cans in the cupboard facing exactly in the same direction. This is a good opportunity to explain that it is not a good idea to get your information from Hollywood. In the movie, the man's wife lived in fear of not keeping the home according to the compulsive standards of her OCD husband. Early in the movie, he viciously beats her for failing to do so. In reality, OCD and violent behavior have no relationship. I have never met an individual with OCD who became violent when his or her spouse did not cooperate with his or her compulsive behaviors. The character's desire for things to be a certain way was an accurate example, however.

I have worked with many people who positioned certain items in their office or home so that they were pointing in a certain direction, positioned equidistant from each side of the desk, etc. In the previous chapter, I described the need for symmetry or exactness as a type of obsession. Ordering and arranging compulsions are often the behavioral manifestation of this obsession. As I mentioned in the last chapter, I worked with one patient who would resist starting each session until she straightened all the pictures and diplomas on my walls and positioned the items on my coffee table so that they were exactly symmetrical in their arrangement. At times, I asked her if we could leave it "out of order" just to see what would happen. Try as she would, the precipitous rise in her anxiety was visible until she could no longer tolerate it, at which point she would reach down to the coffee table in exasperation and re-position the items so that they were "right."

Rubbing, Touching, and Tapping Compulsions

These types of compulsive behaviors involve touching or tapping objects for no better reason than not doing it causes significant anxiety and distress. Often, there is no obvious or logical reason for rubbing, touching or tapping the object. However, *not* doing it can cause a nagging or persistent preoccupation that it *should* have been done, and the OCD sufferers fear that if they don't touch, rub, or tap the object, they will never be able to get the thought out of their head. They reason that it is easier to give in and touch the object than to risk being forever tormented by the thoughts. Of course, the thoughts will not continue forever, but almost no one with OCD is willing to "wait it out."

Compulsive Confessing

Confession of sin is a normal part of the Christian life. Consequently, there is much confusion regarding the difference between healthy confession and the type of compulsive confession that is characteristic of the Christian with OCD. I will discuss this in more detail in chapter 5. However, the type of confession I am talking about here is not the type of confession referred to in scripture. It is primarily a need to seek reassurance from others out of a concern that one has done something wrong when, in fact, they have not. Often this compulsion involves reciting a laundry list of everything the person thinks they may have done that may have harmed someone; hurt someone's feelings; or fallen under the category of immoral behavior.

This compulsion is common among young children who suffer from OCD. Young children with OCD often tell their parents that they have "lied" about something. One youngster upset his parents terribly when he frequently "confessed" to his parents that he had told a lie. His parents, who were well-intended but uneducated about OCD, felt very concerned about the moral development of their son. When asked what he had lied about, the youngster usually would talk about answering a question of preference, but then wondered if he had been "honest" because he was not sure if that was his preference. For example, his teacher asked him what his favorite food was and he told her pizza. He later realized that he also liked hot dogs and began to wonder if he liked hot dogs more than he liked pizza. If that were true, then he reasoned that he had lied to his teacher. To deal with the anxiety and guilt, he needed to confess to his parents. What the youngster really wanted to hear was reassurance that he had not lied, and that he could stop worrying.

Another middle-school student I worked with frequently felt the need to share with his parents at the end of the day every thought that he had throughout the day that may have been "dirty." Since the child was entering puberty and sexual thoughts were frequent, the child was plagued by feelings of anxiety and guilt that his thoughts were "dirty." It was excruciating and embarrassing to share these thoughts with his parents; however, his need to hear that his thoughts were "O.K." was paramount.

Blinking or Staring Compulsions
These types of compulsions involve blinking a certain number of times or in a certain pattern. It may also involve staring at an object or person for a certain number of seconds. Often,

these intervals of blinking and staring are interchanged in a particular pattern. One young man told me that when he was bothered by a thought of something bad happening, he "neutralized" the thought by staring at an object while counting to 33, then blinking three sets of three times. This made him feel that the thought would not happen.

Counting Compulsions

Counting is a common compulsion among people with OCD. It can be severe as in the case of the man who felt the need to count everything in his environment. Or it can be less severe. For example, I know many individuals who compulsively count the stairs as they walk up or down them or count the number of stoplights on the way to work or school. In each case, however, the need to count is compulsive and is accompanied by anxiety if they do not count.

Self-Mutilation Compulsions

While less common, some compulsions involve inflicting self-harm. OCD sufferers have been known to cut, scratch, or even burn themselves compulsively. This should be differentiated from actual suicide attempts that are efforts to literally cause death. Self-mutilation compulsions are experienced as a strong urge to do something that causes non-fatal harm. The person describes a feeling that if they do not engage in the behavior, they will not be able to stop thinking about it to the point that it could literally make them insane.

Compulsive behaviors take many forms. Usually, a person with OCD engages in several different types of compulsive behaviors. Compulsions may be directly related to specific obsessive thoughts or they may appear to be random. However, they always serve to prevent or reduce anxious feelings.

THREE

What Causes OCD?

Like many disorders in the field of mental health, we have a limited understanding of the biological causes of OCD. Fortunately, our knowledge of this disorder has expanded greatly over the past few decades. For example, multiple studies have strongly indicated that OCD is at least partially a genetic illness. In other words, OCD tends to run in families, and a predisposition for the disorder is inherited. Researchers have found that on average, if a person has OCD, the chance that a first-degree relative (e.g., parent, sibling, or child) will have the disorder is in the range of 10 to 25 percent. This rate is much higher than would be expected for a disorder that affects approximately 2 percent of the general population. Perhaps the most convincing evidence for the genetic nature of OCD comes from twin studies. In order to evaluate whether a disorder is familial, researchers compare concordance rates of fraternal and monozygotic twins. Monozygotic (or identical) twins are twins who are derived from the same fertilized egg. In other words, they are formed at the union of one sperm and one ovum. Simply put, monozygotic twins have matching genes; they are essentially genetic clones of one another. Fraternal twins, on the other hand, result from different sperms meeting different ovums. They are no more genetically alike than regular siblings. Concordance rates refer to the percentage of twins who share a disorder. If a disorder has a strong heretability index (i.e., is likely to be inherited), then it stands to reason that if one monozygotic twin has the disorder, there is a higher likelihood that the other twin will have it as well. It would be expected that this likelihood is higher than the likelihood that fraternal twins would share the disorder. Twin studies show that this is indeed the case. Several studies have shown that when an identical twin has OCD, the other twin has OCD approximately 67 percent of the time. However, when a fraternal twin has OCD, the other twin has OCD approximately 47 percent of the time.

Many studies have examined the question of whether OCD is an inherited disorder. At this point, genetic researchers have suggested that OCD is approximately 60 percent genetically caused. This means that OCD definitely runs in families, and that the chances that one may develop OCD are higher if biological relatives also have the disorder. However, like most biological disorders, having OCD does not guarantee that a family member (even a child or sibling) will have OCD. We believe that for many disorders, one inherits a greater predisposition for a disorder and that other variables interact with that vulnerability to determine whether the disorder develops. Let me offer an analogy. If heart disease is partially genetic (which it is believed by many to be), then a person with a strong family history of heart disease should avoid the external risk factors (such as obesity; high blood pressure; smoking; and a sedentary lifestyle) which may interact with that vulnerability to cause heart disease. An individual with a lower genetic predisposition may be able to tolerate the risk factors longer or at a greater level without manifesting heart disease.

We believe the same is true for OCD; that is, a person seems to inherit a predisposition or vulnerability for the disorder that may interact with other variables (e.g., stress) to determine whether the disorder manifests clinically.

Other advances in the scientific study of the brain have offered a much greater understanding of the neurological causes of OCD. Researchers study the brain using several different methods. For example, brain scans help us to draw "maps" of the brain in order to understand how specific regions are involved in symptoms and behaviors. This area of science is known as brain imaging. One type of brain imaging involves injecting a substance into the bloodstream that is labeled with a radioactive isotope. These techniques are known as positron emission tomography (PET scans) or single-photon emission computed tomography (SPECT scans). The substance is usually a compound like a sugar, which is the source of brain nourishment. The sugar travels to the area or areas of the brain that are working hardest, and sophisticated radiology equipment takes a picture of the brain showing where the substance has settled. This type of image clearly shows what areas of the brain are involved in specific functions. For example, if subjects are scanned while reading a book, the image shows that the visual centers near the back of the brain "light up" because the radioactive-labeled sugar has traveled to that area of the brain. If the subject is scanned while listening to music, the auditory centers of the brain light up. These studies are extremely helpful to our understanding of the role of specific regions of the brain.

Another type of brain imaging is known as magnetic resonance imaging (MRI). In this type of study, the brain is imaged by measuring the energy that is emitted by subatomic particles. The image produced is a picture of the structures of the brain, which is used to compare differences between the brains of individuals. In clinical practice, MRI scans help to locate brain abnormalities such as damage caused by strokes or the location of tumors in the brain.

The findings of these types of studies have shown that two areas of the brain seem clearly implicated in OCD: the basal ganglia and the orbital frontal region of the brain. These areas of the brain seem to be over-stimulated in people who suffer from OCD even when they are at rest. These areas of the brain are also intensely active when a person with OCD is engaged in a compulsive ritual. Further evidence for the role of these regions comes from the fact that these areas of the brain show "normal" functioning when the person is treated for OCD with medication or behavior therapy (to be discussed later).

A better understanding of how these areas of the brain work adds to our understanding of why these areas of the brain are involved. The basal ganglia is actually an area of the brain that contains several structures, including the caudate nucleus, putamen, and substantia nigra. These structures work together to control initiation and modulation of movement and to process and filter information that is fed back to help control behavior and thinking. In animal studies, damage to the basal ganglia is linked to the repeated performance of behaviors that resemble compulsive rituals. Several studies involving human subjects have shown that cases of brain injury that led to physical injury limited to the basal ganglia have led to the sudden onset of OCD symptoms. Additionally, three separate disorders of the basal ganglia have been associated with the onset of OCD symptoms in patients. History shows that the world flu pandemic between 1917 and 1926 often resulted in a brain infection known as Von Economo's encephalitis. The condition resulted in damage to the basal ganglia. Symptoms of the illness included obsessions and compulsions, and counting rituals were particularly common. Another disease known as Huntington's disease also includes the symptoms of obsessive cleaning and checking in the early stages of the illness. In Hungtington's disease, brain damage is restricted largely to the basal ganglia. Finally, Sydenham's Chorea is a rare, neurological disorder that results from damage to the basal ganglia. In this disorder, antibodies produced by the immune system to combat invading bacteria mistake basal ganglia nerve cells as bacteria and destroy them. This disorder results in abnormal movements as well as the development of OCD.

The other primary region of the brain involved in OCD is the orbital frontal region, an area located behind the forehead. The primary functions of this area of the brain include filtering, prioritizing, and organizing information received by the brain; inhibiting responses to irrelevant stimuli; engaging in logical and consequence-based decision making; and regulating movements and complex behaviors activated by the basal ganglia.

Perhaps the most useful understanding of the role of the brain in OCD is the knowledge we have of the role of the neurotransmitter serotonin in the development of OCD symptoms. Neurotransmitters are chemicals in the brain that are crucial for communication between nerve cells in the brain. There are many different types of neurotransmitters in the brain, and serotonin is only one of many. The brain is comprised of billions of nerve cells known as neurons. These cells are interconnected and project from one area of the brain to another. This is the manner in which different regions of the brain communicate with one another. For example, when I ask my son to "Pass the salt" at the dinner table, his brain must accurately hear and interpret the words (auditory region); locate the salt on the table (visual region); and transfer the message to the part of the brain that enables him to actually pick up the salt and hand it to me (motor region). While this is dramatically oversimplified, it illustrates that even the simplest action requires different regions of the brain to communicate with each other. This can only occur if the neurons, which are interconnected throughout the brain like a series of phone wires, are accurately communicating with one another. These neurons don't actually touch, but instead, meet at a small space called a synapse or synaptic cleft. The way these neurons communicate is by the following method:

1. The "sender" neuron releases a chemical (a neurotransmitter) into the space known as the synapse. Think of a quarterback throwing a pass to a receiver.
2. The "receiver" neuron contains receptor sites that "catch" the neurotransmitter from the "sender" neuron. Think of a receiver preparing to catch the ball.
3. Once enough of the neurotransmitter from the "sender" finds its way to the receptor sites on the "receiver" (the pass is complete), the receiver neuron is "activated" which means the message has been sent and the message can be transmitted via an electrical impulse

down the line to the next neuron.

4. There is usually an excess of the neurotransmitter left over in the space or synapse. At this point, the "sender" neuron releases a transporter protein into the synapse to re-package the excess neurotransmitter and bring it back into the "sender" neuron to be used later. This is much like a natural re-cycling process of the brain.

We know that in people who suffer from OCD, there appears to be a deficiency of the neurotransmitter serotonin in the brain. The best evidence for the serotonin deficiency theory comes from the many well-designed medication studies for the treatment of OCD. These studies consistently show that treating patients with OCD with medications that increase serotonin activity in the brain significantly reduces the symptoms of OCD. In fact, the studies show that treating OCD with serotonin enhancing drugs is effective in the vast majority of patients. There is also evidence that giving a patient with OCD a substance mCPP (m-chlorophenylpiperazine) that works by opposing serotonin activity in the brain actually makes obsessions and compulsions worse. Interestingly, when the substance is given to people who do not have OCD, no changes are seen. A more thorough discussion of the treatment of OCD using medications will be discussed in a later chapter of this book.

Consistent with the previously discussed research on brain regions, it is interesting that relatively high concentrations of serotonin are present in the basal ganglia.

Evidence from scientific studies clearly supports the conclusion that OCD is a biological condition that results from specific abnormalities in certain regions of the brain and an imbalance in the neurotransmitter serotonin. OCD also has a genetic component, and it appears that people inherit the biological predisposition to OCD. These findings should remove any stigma associated with OCD. It is clear that OCD is *not* a problem that is caused by unconscious conflicts; a psychological "weakness"; or any kind of demonic involvement or spiritual oppression. It is a disorder of brain functioning. Fortunately, this helps us to understand how to treat OCD more effectively.

FOUR

Obsessive-Compulsive Disorder in Children and Teenagers

OCD is a disorder that affects children as well as adults. It has been estimated that approximately 1.9 percent of children and adolescents will develop OCD. Several studies place the average age of onset of OCD in children at around 10.2 years of age. However, many children show symptoms of OCD at a much earlier age. In children, boys tend to show symptoms earlier than girls (by a ratio of about 3:2). It is believed by most experts in the field that OCD is frequently undiagnosed in children, even by mental health professionals. The two main reasons for this are (1) children are very good at "hiding" their symptoms in order to appear normal; and (2) most adults do not recognize the signs and symptoms of OCD in children.

It is rare for children to articulate their symptoms to other adults. Many children accept their symptoms as "normal" and may not be aware that others do not have the same types of obsessive thoughts or engage in the same types of compulsive behaviors. For those children who do recognize their symptoms as an anomaly, they may be embarrassed to discuss them with others. Furthermore, children typically do not discuss being plagued by obsessive thoughts.

It is also difficult for many parents and teachers to

recognize the symptoms of childhood OCD as being a disorder. Many children show some occasional superstitious thinking or some mild compulsive types of behavior. What parent has not had a child refuse to wear a particular pair of pants or struggled with a young child who refused to eat something because it "has weird stuff in it?" Therefore, it can be easy to dismiss genuine OCD symptoms as being a normal part of child behavior. In chapters 1 and 2, I listed some of the more common types of obsessions and compulsions. Children and teenagers can and do exhibit symptoms in these categories. In her excellent book, *Freeing Your Child from Obsessive-Compulsive Disorder,* Dr. Tamar Chansky offers a very helpful list of "red flags" that may help adults to recognize the possibility that a child may be suffering from OCD. Her lists contain some of the following signs:

For Contamination Obsessions/Compulsions:
- long trips to the bathroom
- multiple and/or long showers
- excessive use of soap, toothpaste, towels, toilet paper
- avoiding doorknobs, light switches, furniture
- keeping food or silverware separate from other family members
- inspecting silverware to make sure it is clean
- frequent questioning about cleanliness or contamination
- excessive concern over germs; illness; etc.
- refusing to share items that others have touched
- chapped or bleeding skin (especially hands)
- inspecting items (food, furniture, etc.) for signs of contamination

For Checking Compulsions:
- checking or changing underwear to make sure it is dry
- checking to make sure things are off or locked
- asking frequent questions that are seeking reassurance

For Obsessive Doubting and Religious Obsessions:
- urgency about prayers
- fears that they may have used profanity or raised their middle finger
- excessive apologizing for "no good reason"
- needing to confess minor transgressions—thoughts, actions
- indecisiveness, fear of terrible consequences for making the "wrong choice"[1]

While Dr. Chansky's list is not exhaustive, it is extremely helpful in pointing out that children with OCD often manifest their disorder through behaviors that may not be classic compulsive behaviors. None of the behaviors listed above are considered classic compulsive behaviors. And it should be noted that the presence of one or even a few of these alone are not pathognomonic of OCD. However, if a child exhibits these behaviors, it could be a "red flag" as Dr. Chansky suggests. Furthermore, as I mentioned before, children typically do not discuss being plagued by obsessive thoughts.

Looks can be deceptive—OCD manifesting as a behavior problem:
In my clinical experience, children and teenagers with OCD are often inaccurately diagnosed or characterized as having a behavior problem. By now, you have an idea of how difficult it

is for an individual with OCD to resist the urge to carry out a compulsive act. For children with OCD, they often feel forced to carry through with a particular compulsive act or series of behaviors even though doing so may result in negative consequences. For example, Cheryl was a high-school girl who was in daily battles with her parents over her "tardiness problem." Cheryl was late for school every morning. Her parents tried everything to get her to leave the house on time for school. By the time they got into my office, tempers were high, and the morning battles were escalating to full-scale wars. Her parents were baffled: Cheryl got up plenty early; she had no ostensible reason for being late; and she had suffered myriad restrictions and punishments for her "disobedience and lack of responsibility." Why was Cheryl unable to get herself out the door on time in the morning?

In an individual meeting with me, Cheryl began to describe getting "stuck" in her morning routine. Her pattern started sounding familiar, so I started asking questions about certain types of compulsive behaviors. As I began to ask more specific questions about "thoughts that pop into your head that make you feel bad" and "feeling like you have to do things in a certain way or something bad may happen," Cheryl appeared to be both delighted and perplexed that I seemed to "understand" what she was going through. Cheryl was suffering from classic symptoms of OCD that made her morning routine a tortuous series of rituals and "do overs" that resulted in her taking an inordinate amount of time to get everything just right before she could leave the house.

For example, as soon as she woke up, she described the need to think a certain thought "in just the right way" before she could get out of bed. If she did not think the right thought in the right way, she feared that something bad would happen to her that day (e.g., she may get into trouble). Because Cheryl was a conscientious young girl, the thought of getting into trouble was terrifying. It was also irrational since she had never really been in trouble at school in her entire life. As with most obsessive thoughts, however, the fear was genuine and intense. Getting the right thought could take up to 10 minutes of real effort. As she brushed her teeth, she had to brush in a particular pattern for a particular number of times on each side. Additionally, she would have to turn the water on and off a certain number of times before finishing. Any misstep in the series would require her to start the entire series over from the beginning. Putting on her make-up was also a Herculean effort as she had to make sure that she had "exactly the right amount" on each side of her face (making it symmetrical). When I asked how she knew when this was accomplished, she replied (characteristic of most sufferers of OCD), "I just know when it's right." Finally, getting dressed was a grueling ordeal. Clothes had to fit just right—not too tight and not too loose. Of course, everything had to be symmetrical which could take several minutes to accomplish. And finally, similar to her need to think the right thought before getting out of bed, Cheryl had to think "good thoughts" as she put on each article of clothing. If she doubted that she thought the right thought, she felt the need to take it off and put it back on again until she was satisfied that she had, indeed, thought the right thought as she put on the article of clothing.

As you may imagine, Cheryl's morning ritual was exhausting. By the time she was ready for school, her parents were furious, Cheryl felt terrible, and the day was off to a horrendous beginning. You may ask why Cheryl didn't simply explain to her parents that she was engaged in all of these rituals which were making her late every morning. However, Cheryl told me that she feared that her parents would think that she was crazy. In fact, Cheryl had wondered many times if she actually *was* going crazy. After all, she realized that these behaviors were irrational and were causing her and her family tremendous turmoil. She frequently asked herself why she simply didn't just stop. Unfortunately, failure in her early attempts to "make the next morning different" and resist the compulsive behaviors reinforced to her that it was hopeless. She simply became too anxious and started worrying when she skipped a ritual. Her mounting anxiety inevitably would force her to return and complete the compulsive behavior before being able to leave her house.

Fortunately, Cheryl gave me permission to share with her parents that she was suffering from OCD. It was vital that they understood what OCD was, and that Cheryl was not the least bit crazy. In fact, she was a bright and lovely young girl who was tormented by OCD. Her parents were relieved and grateful to finally understand the reason for Cheryl's morning difficulties. The proper understanding of the problem allowed Cheryl and her parents to reframe the problem from one of "disobedience and lack of responsibility" (a problem *with* Cheryl) to a problem of OCD (a problem that *affected* Cheryl). This paradigm shift almost immediately resulted in a change in the family climate from one of anger and hostility to one of compassion, understanding, and a resolve to work together as a team to beat the OCD.

More masquerading—OCD manifesting as ADHD:

Another frequent misdiagnosis for children with OCD is a diagnosis of attention-deficit hyperactivity Disorder (ADHD). While ADHD is the correct clinical or technical term for children and teens that have problems with sustained attention and focus and/or impulsivity and disinhibition, this disorder is still known as and referred to by its older label of attention-deficit disorder (ADD). I will use the current clinical term ADHD in this book. Being plagued by obsessive thoughts is extremely distracting. In fact, obsessive thoughts are by nature preoccupying. In addition, mental compulsions (e.g., counting; thinking certain thoughts; compulsive praying; etc.) can make it all but impossible to be focused on anything else going on around you. For children in school, OCD can make it extraordinarily difficult to concentrate on school work. Additionally, frequent compulsive rituals can cause a child to appear fidgety and restless.

Another way in which OCD negatively affects academic performance is through compulsions such as re-writing and re-reading. Many students describe OCD causes them to feel that they have to re-read entire paragraphs or pages because they may have thought a wrong thought as they read; or perhaps they fear that they may have not read a word and they must go back and make sure they read each word carefully. Some students describe the need to make letters look a certain way when writing. They become very anxious if they think they did not form a letter "correctly" and they frequently erase and re-write in order to "get it right." Then there are those students with OCD who have a need to turn in "perfect" work and cannot turn work in at all because it is never "good enough."

For students with OCD, school is just one more place where the symptoms can interfere with life. James was a middle-school student who was referred to me by the faculty of his school. James was a bright young boy who had always done well in school. He recently started slipping in his grades, and his parents and teachers were baffled by the decline in his school work. James was historically a very conscientious worker. In fact, his parents described him as usually being more responsible than his peers with regard to school work. Recently, however, James was not working up to his potential. He was handing in work late, and sometimes not at all. Teachers were using words like, "distracted"; "not focused"; "spacey"; and "preoccupied" to describe his behavior in class. His teachers were wondering if James was showing signs of ADHD and felt that perhaps the extra demands of middle school were causing his symptoms to "catch up with him."

I conducted an interview and found no strong evidence of symptoms consistent with ADHD in his early childhood. His parents described a responsible young man who was a bit rigid in his ways of doing things. I sent some behavioral rating scales to his teachers and asked his parents to complete some similar instruments. When I collected and scored these instruments, the scales that are normally elevated in students who have attention problems were, in fact, significantly elevated suggesting that James was having trouble with focus in class. However, another scale was also elevated on both the teacher and parent form—the *Anxiety* scale. This elevation suggested that James was also showing some symptoms associated with anxiety in school and at home.

I followed up with James and started asking about symptoms of OCD. James acknowledged that he did have thoughts and images that randomly popped into his head and caused him great distress. A frequent thought that bothered him was of something happening to his father. James' father suffered some rather serious health problems early in James' life; however, his father had been healthy and asymptomatic for years. Nonetheless, James worried excessively about his father's health. These images and thoughts were followed by a need to do things to "protect" his father. For example, James was a devout Christian young man who felt that because God existed as a trinity of Father, Son, and Holy Spirit, the number 3 was holy and protective. Consequently, James did things in 3's when plagued by these thoughts. For instance, if he glanced at an object in his environment, he made sure that he looked at it 3 times out of each eye before he could move on to something else. He also silently said specific prayers about his father—some of them lasting several minutes. These prayers were recited 3 times each. When he was plagued by these obsessive thoughts concerning his father's health, he even felt the need to count his words so that when he was finished making a statement or asking a question, the total count of his spoken words was a number divisible by 3. This often resulted in clumsy speech with words added to statements and questions.

Needless to say, James was spending a great deal of time focused on things other than his teachers and his schoolwork. When his OCD was in full force, James found it impossible to retain anything that was being discussed in class. It was important to understand that James was not paying attention in the classroom. However, it appeared that his attention problems were primarily due to OCD rather than ADHD.

I recall another young man who was brought to me after having been diagnosed and treated by another professional. Steve was diagnosed in 4th grade with ADHD and was placed on stimulant medication to treat the symptoms. While it seemed to help a bit initially, by the time Steve was beginning 5th grade, he seemed worse. He was still distracted and he seemed to be more emotional, crying easily and becoming irritable over small things. He also worried frequently. A thorough assessment revealed that Steve had classic OCD. These symptoms were causing him to have difficulty with participating in the classroom and with work completion. The stimulant seemed to increase his anxiety levels and actually appeared to be exacerbating his OCD symptoms.

While more and more data are being published to suggest that OCD and ADHD do co-exist in the same students frequently, I always make sure that if a student is showing any symptoms of attention problems, OCD symptoms have been addressed before making a diagnosis of ADHD. It is not unusual for students suffering from both ADHD and OCD to receive simultaneous treatment for both conditions. However, I believe that anxiety levels must be decreased and that OCD symptoms must be under control before one can accurately determine the student's ability to concentrate and focus.

The downward spiral—when OCD leads to depression:
Some researchers have found that up to 25 percent of children with OCD develop symptoms of clinical depression. I have seen many children and teens who were brought to me for symptoms of depression only to find that they struggled with OCD for months, and in some cases, years before they

started showing signs of depression. Imagine being a child plagued by intrusive disturbing thoughts that you could not control. Imagine feeling that you "had to" engage in frequent behaviors that were time consuming and nonpleasurable and fearing that if you did not do the behavior "just so" it could result in something terrible happening to a loved one. Imagine believing that you may be responsible for something awful happening and that you may have to live with the guilt for the rest of your life. Now, imagine that you believe there is no hope for you ever changing—that every effort you have made to resist these compulsive behaviors or to stop the barrage of anxiety producing thoughts and images has failed. It is not difficult to understand why children and teens with OCD can become depressed.

A discussion of childhood and adolescent depression is far beyond the scope of this book. However, let me offer a few comments that clarify what depression may look like in a child or teenager. Depression is a frequently used term in our lexicon. We use the word depression descriptively to refer to even normal feelings of sadness. For example, "I'm depressed today because my tennis match was rained out," or, "I think Bob is depressed because his computer crashed and he lost the report he was working on." Using the word depression in this way is different from what we refer to as a clinical depression. Clinical depression is a biological condition that also involves imbalances in neurotransmitters and results in a definite change in mood and behavior. While clinical depression can manifest differently from child to child, some common symptoms include:

- a loss of interest in previously enjoyed activities or relationships
- a lack of motivation or drive
- social isolation or withdrawal
- irritability
- obvious sadness (tearfulness; rarely smiles; no joy)
- a noticeable drop in grades or performance in other areas of life
- lack of concern about appearance
- talks about wanting to die or killing self (an indication of severe depression)
- fatigue (easily tired; never has much energy)
- sleep disturbances (either sleeps excessively or may have trouble sleeping—insomnia)
- eating disturbances (either eats more than usual or suddenly has no appetite)
- doesn't enjoy things the way he or she used to—inability to experience pleasure

If a child or teen exhibits several of these symptoms for more than 2 weeks, it could be a sign of clinical depression. A child or teenager who suffers from OCD for a prolonged period of time without any help may be at an increased risk of becoming clinically depressed.

The slippery slope—substance abuse and OCD:
Adolescents today grow up in a world in which alcohol and drug abuse is not uncommon. Statistics from the Center for Disease Control in Atlanta, Georgia, indicate that by the time a student is in 12th grade, 88 percent have tried alcohol and approximately 61 percent of seniors report that they have

used alcohol at least once in the past 30 days. By the time a student reaches 12th grade, 58 percent state that they have tried marijuana, and almost ⅓ of high school seniors report having used marijuana at least once in the preceding 30 days.[2] For teenagers suffering from untreated OCD, the risk of substance abuse is elevated. Many teenagers I have worked with have shared that the use of alcohol or other drugs such as marijuana provide temporary relief from the anxiety caused by OCD. In fact, some teenagers have shared that they are virtually free of obsessive thoughts and the need to engage in compulsive behaviors as long as they have a "buzz" (the effects of an intoxicant).

Professionals refer to this as "self-medicating" symptoms. In other words, teenagers may select illegal substances in order to make their symptoms temporarily disappear, or at least, decrease in intensity for a brief period of time. In my experience, alcohol and marijuana are the drugs of choice for teenagers who turn to substance abuse to obtain relief from OCD. Both of these substances are central nervous system depressants and seem to produce an antianxiety effect on the individual. These substances have a powerful effect on the brain and produce acute effects. For a teenager suffering from symptoms of OCD, the powerful contrast of a sense of relaxation and freedom from obsessive thoughts and compulsive urges compared to their high levels of anxiety and the burden of OCD symptoms is incredible. Because they experience such a relief from their symptoms, these drugs have a very strong appeal. As with all substance abuse problems, the negative effects of using these drugs are typically not evident at first. It often takes a while before the teenager begins to see or experience the negative effects of using alcohol or other drugs (e.g., negative effects on school performance; possible increased levels of depression with extended use; developing dependency on the substance; problems with important relationships; physical risks involved with using drugs and alcohol; getting into legal trouble; etc.).

Furthermore, as with most substances like alcohol and marijuana, the teenager develops tolerance to the substance. This means that the teenager will need increasing amounts of the substance in order to achieve the same effects. For example, a teen may experience a significant sense of relief after drinking only one or two beers the first time. However, as they develop tolerance for alcohol, they may need 5 or 6 to achieve the same level of relief that they experienced the first time they drank. This gradual increase in usage can lead to dependency and addiction. I have worked with teenagers and adults who struggled with a dual diagnosis: OCD and a substance abuse problem.

It is important to understand that OCD may show up and affect children and teenagers in ways that are different from adult manifestation of the disorder. I will discuss special considerations in treating OCD in children and adolescents in chapter 8.

FIVE

Spiritual Issues and OCD

In Chapter 3 we discussed the biological basis of OCD. Even though research has taught us much about the physiological causes of OCD, it remains a disorder that is frequently misunderstood by the general population. As a psychologist who works frequently with Christians, I am surprised to see how misunderstood and often how mishandled OCD is within the Christian community. Because obsessions and compulsions can have religious or spiritual themes, there are some within the Church who see OCD as a "spiritual problem." I have even spoken with some who claim that the symptoms of OCD are caused by demonic oppression or even demonic possession. For a Christian already tormented by anxiety caused by OCD, having someone suggest that these symptoms are caused by demonic involvement can literally push them over the edge.

I've seen too many Christians with OCD who have been harmed by well-intended church members who suggested that if they only had more faith or prayed more, their symptoms would disappear. I've also heard far too many stories of Christians with OCD who were told by church members (or even church officials) that their symptoms were present because of "unconfessed sin" in their lives. This type of uneducated advice can be extraordinarily harmful to someone with OCD whose symptoms include obsessive concerns that their normal, everyday behaviors are sinful; fears of not being a "good enough Christian"; or fears of being condemned because of bad thoughts. For example, I worked with a young man named Scott who was constantly tormented by anxiety and guilt. He described almost constantly feeling as though he "might have lied" to someone during the course of a normal day. Since Scott believed that lying was a sin, he was constantly praying for forgiveness, and he frequently returned to the people to whom he feared he lied in order to clarify himself and to ask for their forgiveness. When I asked for an example, Scott offered the following: "This morning, I stopped by a bakery and ordered a bagel. The woman behind the counter asked if I liked cream cheese on my bagel. I told her no. After I left, I started to think that sometimes I do put cream cheese on my bagel. Today I didn't want cream cheese on my bagel, but sometimes I do. Therefore, I felt like I lied to her because when she asked me if I liked cream cheese on my bagel I said no, and that is a lie since there are times when I do." When I asked what he did in response to his thoughts, he replied, "After I left and had driven about 2 miles away from the bakery, the guilt overwhelmed me and I had to turn around and go back. I went back inside the bakery and tried to explain to the woman that I lied to her about not liking cream cheese on my bagel. She looked at me like I was crazy. Maybe I am." To tell this young man that his problems would disappear if he simply prayed more, had more faith, and got rid of all of the unconfessed sin in his life would be inaccurate, unethical, and extremely harmful.

If you suffer from OCD, or if you know someone who suffers from OCD, please understand that *OCD is a biological condition caused primarily by an imbalance in brain chemistry.* It is *not* caused by demonic involvement. To suggest otherwise is as ridiculous as suggesting that individuals who suffer from near-sightedness, diabetes, or crooked teeth are possessed by demons or suffer their malady because of sin in their lives.

The symptoms of OCD often do manifest with religious or spiritual themes. This is particularly true of Christians and people of other faiths for whom their beliefs are an integral part of their lives. Here are a few examples.

Obsessions over Committing the "Unpardonable Sin"

One of the more frequent obsessive thoughts/fears for Christians suffering from OCD is the fear that they may have "committed the unpardonable sin." They may also express this as the fear that they may have "blasphemed the Holy Ghost." Almost without exception, these individuals quote the verse from Matthew 12:31 (*NKJV*) that reads, "Therefore I say to you, every sin and blasphemy will be forgiven men, but the blasphemy against the Spirit will not be forgiven men"; or the verse from Mark 3:28-29 (*NKJV*) that reads, "'Assuredly, I say to you, all sins will be forgiven the sons of men, and whatever blasphemies they may utter; but he who blasphemes against the Holy Spirit never has forgiveness, but is subject to eternal condemnation'—because they said, 'He has an unclean spirit.'" These verses serve as the source of torment for many Christians with OCD who are incessantly tormented with the thought or fear that they may have somehow brought eternal condemnation upon themselves by "committing blasphemy against the Spirit." Few of these people can tell you clearly what they actually did that qualifies as blasphemy against the Spirit.

Theological scholars have debated the meaning of these scripture verses. However, many leading scholars suggest that these passages refer to rejecting any and all promptings of the Spirit of God that convict mankind of his sinfulness and need for salvation. It is ironic that the very individuals who feel "condemned" are applying a passage of scripture that refers to those who feel *no conviction* from the Holy Spirit. Unfortunately, even the most articulate and educated expert on the scriptures would have a difficult time convincing most Christians who suffer from this and other religious obsessions. Many people with OCD simply use *emotional reasoning* (a term that refers to reaching a conclusion based on how one feels rather than on facts and data). Therefore, the OCD sufferer describes that they *feel* unforgiven and condemned, *therefore,* they *must be.*

Obsessing About Impulsive Sinful Acts

Another frequent obsessive thought or fear is that of doing something impulsively that is beyond the person's control and that is inappropriate or embarrassing. Patients have described the fear that they will stand up in a crowded room and scream some obscenity; make a sexual gesture in public; or disrobe in front of others to name a few. For Christians, these obsessions can be extremely anxiety producing. I've talked with many Christians who described the fear that they will do something terribly inappropriate, especially during a church service.

George was a thirty-nine-year-old man who sang in his church's choir. He enjoyed music for as long as he could remember. George was quite talented musically and had a fine voice. As a young adult, he even sang in an amateur rock-and-roll band. His lifestyle during those years was somewhat stereo-typical of what you might imagine for a lead singer of a rock-and-roll band. He engaged in many indiscriminant sexual encounters; got into more than his share of brawls; and spent lots of money and time pursuing a drug- or alcohol-induced state of altered consciousness. George responded to an evan-gelist's invitation to accept Christ in his late 20's, and he could pinpoint the date, place, and time that he was "saved." George did not struggle with the message of the Gospel or the securi-ty of his salvation. In fact, George was assured that he was loved by God and that he was completely forgiven of all that he had ever done in his "lost" days as well as any sins that he may commit in the future. This was, in fact, one of the reasons that he enjoyed singing in the choir. George was truly grateful for all that God had done for him, and he looked forward to each Sunday when he could join the other members of his choir in singing songs of praise, worship, and thanksgiving to the God that loved him enough to find him and save him from his sinful lifestyle. Unfortunately, George suffered from OCD which made his experience of singing in the choir a source of terror. George described the fear that during a song, he would suddenly shout out the vilest obscenities one could imagine. His image was complete with the vision of the entire church becoming silent while everyone stared at George in complete horror and disbelief. George found this image so disconcerting; he began to worry as soon as the weekend arrived. He began to dread Sunday mornings, and he was relieved when church was over and he realized that he made it one more week without "shocking the congregation." The truth was that George had never acted impulsively in church in his life. In fact, George did not even use profanity in his everyday conversation. When I asked George what precise words he feared he may shout from the stage, he had tremendous difficulty even saying them out loud. It was obvious that George was not a man of profane language. However, his obsessive thoughts caused so much anxiety that he had feigned illness on more than one Sunday morning to avoid singing in the choir, and he was actually contemplating quitting the choir altogether.

Disturbing Religious Imagery

Christians with OCD often describe suffering from intrusive images of things that are deeply disturbing and anxiety producing. These images often involve religious symbols or images that are distorted or paired with some stimuli that are inconsistent with what the religious image means to them.

After I completed my internship, I was fortunate to obtain a position working as a psychologist in an inpatient treatment facility that offered a program for patients seeking professional help using a Christian treatment approach. The program was appealing to those of the Christian faith since some Christians are reticent to seek help from professionals. Many Christians fear that non-Christian mental health professionals will attack their spiritual beliefs, or perhaps worse, they may try to treat them with a "secular approach" which some Christians are certain will be not only "non-Christian," but blatantly "anti-Christian." Let me make a brief personal statement regarding this issue. There are many non-Christian mental health professionals who honor and respect the faith and beliefs of Christians. They may not share your faith, but they will respect it. These same professionals are highly competent and can offer valuable help to people who suffer from OCD or other problems. Similarly, I have known some Christian psychiatrists, psychologists, and therapists who are poorly trained and would not receive my endorsement as a treating professional. If you are seeking help for OCD, have an honest and open discussion with your doctor or therapist about the importance of your faith. Don't hesitate to ask questions about how the person views your beliefs and how he or she intends to handle issues of spirituality with you. If you are not comfortable with the answers, keep looking. In a like manner, don't assume that because someone advertises as a Christian doctor or therapist, he or she is competent to help you. Ask questions about his or her training and background and about whether he or she has experience working with OCD. Again, if you don't feel comfortable, keep looking.

During my work in the inpatient setting, I led a daily therapy group with the patients on the unit. There was a man in my group named Tom, who was a middle-aged man suffering from tremendous guilt and anxiety. For the first few days of group, Tom sat rather quietly with a furrowed brow. I could tell that he had a lot on his mind, but he rarely shared with the group. Feeling that he should be getting more comfortable with the group members, I asked him to share a bit about why he was in the hospital. Tom reluctantly shared that he was bothered by "bad thoughts" that were becoming so pervasive he was having trouble performing on his job. Expecting him to share that he had thoughts of infidelity or of pilfering from the cash drawer at work, I asked him to share further. He then shared with the group that he often had the image of a cross appear in his mind, followed by an additional image a few seconds later of excrement being splattered on the cross. At times, the image would change. His obsessive image always started with the image of a cross. However, it was quickly followed by something that he thought was bad, and that was completely incongruent with what the cross represented for him. Examples included the image of a cross with an obscenity written over it and the image of a cross with two people having sex underneath it. Because Tom found these images to be so unacceptable and so bizarre, he would never have shared them with the group if I had not pushed him to do so.

Obsessing About Losing One's Salvation

For other Christians suffering from OCD, they obsess over the fear that they may lose their salvation. Janet was a thirty-two-year-old woman who was referred by her pastor. She was a very popular member of her church, volunteering frequently and attending regularly. She was a mother of three young children and seemed to have it all together. However, she described suffering from incredible anxiety and fear that she might lose her salvation. When I asked her why she worried so much about this issue, she cited several scripture verses that caused her to believe that if she "sinned" she would lose her salvation and be in danger of spending an eternity in Hell. For Janet, this obsession led to the development of some compulsive behaviors. It was a rare church service that Janet did not walk down the aisle in order to respond to her pastor's invitation for those who had never placed their faith in Christ to come forward and receive the gift of salvation from God. Janet was typically the first to respond. Her pastor confided in me that while he appreciated Janet's sincerity, her role in the church caused her to be viewed by other congregation members as a leader in the church. Because others looked up to Janet, they began to doubt their own salvation after seeing Janet repeatedly publicly announce her need for salvation. Her pastor told me, "My church members are telling me that if Janet can't be sure of her salvation, then I must be on thin ice as well." While responding to altar calls in her church brought temporary relief from her anxiety, it was only a matter of time before she did or thought something that caused her to fear she had forfeited her salvation. Between church services, Janet developed a ritualistic prayer that she would pray over and over throughout the day that she felt "covered her" until she could get to church and publicly respond to the pastor's invitation for salvation.

Janet's case illustrates three issues that are typical of Christians with OCD. First, many Christians with OCD seem to select specific Bible verses that "support" their fears or obsessive thoughts. Often, these verses are taken out of context, and the greater meaning of the passage from which they are lifted is lost. For Janet, she seemed to have "scriptural tunnel vision." In other words, she would focus on a specific Bible verse, or even part of a verse of scripture that seemed to suggest to her that when she disobeyed God, she immediately lost her salvation and needed to be "re-saved." Janet seemed to miss the message of the gospel found in Romans 5 which tells us that God loves us so much that he allows a way for us to experience total forgiveness for our sinful condition by placing our faith in Christ's death as full payment for our sins (past, present, and future). She missed the message of the *entire* Bible that tells us that our relationship with God is not based upon our "goodness," but on our faith in Christ's deity and sacrificial death as complete payment for our sin. Many Christians fail to grasp the message of the gospel and instead focus on one or two verses that are interpreted outside of the context of the message of grace.

The second issue that Janet's case illustrates is the tenacity with which the Christian with OCD holds firm to their misinterpretation or misapplication of scripture. I recall a gentleman named Rob who suffered from OCD and ruminated incessantly about losing his salvation. His family members went to great lengths to arrange a meeting with a very well-known pastor whom Rob greatly respected. In fact, if this particular pastor was on television, Rob was sure to be there watching. His family reasoned that if Rob could hear directly from this pastor's mouth that he was secure in his relationship with God and that Rob was, indeed, taking certain verses out of context, surely he would feel better and stop obsessing. Unfortunately, Rob was not easily convinced. Rather than accepting a sound and biblically based explanation from a man he greatly admired and respected, Rob came up with myriad questions and "what if's" that eventually left the poor pastor feeling frustrated, exasperated, and hopeless that he could help Rob. The pastor wisely suggested that perhaps Rob needed to talk with a psychologist rather than a pastor. Because the obsessions of the person with OCD are usually not based on logic, they rarely respond to a logical argument. Remember, conclusions are reached based on emotion when a person is using emotional reasoning.

Finally, Janet's case illustrates the issue of religious compulsions, which I will describe in the following section.

Religious Compulsions

Just as obsessions can be related to spiritual issues, compulsive behaviors can take the form of spiritual or religious behaviors. Janet became compulsive regarding behaviors that are generally very normal and healthy for Christians. In fact, some of the things that become compulsive symptoms for the Christian with OCD are actually vital to the life of a Christian if not done compulsively. However, for many Christians with OCD, these behaviors become compulsions.

Compulsive Prayer

All Christians pray. Prayer is a Christian's way of communicating with God. In fact, Jesus taught his disciples to pray frequently through his teachings and his own example. Can the very thing that Jesus taught us to do become a symptom of a disorder? The answer is yes. For many Christians with OCD, prayer becomes a compulsive behavior. It is important to distinguish between genuine, non-compulsive prayer and the type of prayer that is a compulsive behavior. For the purposes of illustrating the difference, allow me to draw a simple analogy: If I want to communicate with my wife when I am at work, I pick up the telephone, place a call to our house, and have a conversation with her. I may ask her to run an errand for me, tell her when I will be home that evening, or simply call to say hello and ask how her day is going. It is always for a specific purpose and the conversation is spontaneous and effortless. After I hang up, I feel good and have enjoyed the brief conversation. Usually, I feel a bit closer to my wife following the conversation. Now, suppose I felt that I "had" to phone her each hour on the hour to tell her that I loved her and that I hoped she had a good day. The motive would not be a desire to connect with her, but rather a "compulsion" to phone. Suppose I felt that if I didn't phone, she may no longer love me, or worse, I believed that if I didn't phone and deliver the message something terrible might happen to her. After a while, the phone calls would become burdensome not only to me, but to my wife as well. I would derive no pleasure from the phone call, and it would be rather insincere and arduous. The first type of call I described would be analogous to the genuine prayers of a Christian (i.e., a sincere attempt to connect with and communicate with God). The latter type of call would be similar to the type of "compulsive praying" that the Christian with OCD engages in. These types of prayers are often rote recitations of specific phrases that are offered to obtain forgiveness, "undo" a bad thought, or prevent something bad from happening. The person feels more of a compulsion to say the prayer rather than a sincere desire to communicate with God. There is little spontaneity, and the person derives little, if any, satisfaction from the prayer. There is no increased sense of intimacy with God following these types of prayers.

Jordan was a fourteen-year-old boy who was brought to me for symptoms of OCD. He was a normally developing adolescent who was typically a good student in a private Christian school. He was raised in a Christian home and attended church with his parents regularly. His teachers felt that he was rapidly falling behind in school and worried that he was having trouble focusing in class. When I spoke with Jordan, he confided in me that he had frequent thoughts of a sexual nature. He described these thoughts as "like a movie scene that crashes into my head. The more I try not to think about them, the stronger they become." I explained to Jordan that at his age, it was perfectly normal to have frequent sexual thoughts and feelings and that there was a huge and important difference between having thoughts that enter your mind and acting on them. However, Jordan felt that these thoughts made him "dirty," and he feared that he would go to Hell if he did not pray a specific prayer of confession each time he had one. There were times when his prayers could barely keep up with his thoughts. He was trapped in a vicious cycle which preoccupied most of his waking moments. It was no wonder that he had gone from a solid A/B student to practically failing every class.

Charlotte was a twenty-year-old college student who saw me for symptoms of OCD. Charlotte's obsessions were primarily about something happening to her family. She loved her parents and little brother dearly and worried constantly that they might be killed in a car accident or some other type of disaster. Each time Charlotte had a thought of something happening to one of her family members, she felt that she had to recite the following prayer verbatim:

"Dear God,
Please place your hands around Mom, Dad, and James. Watch over them and protect them from harm. Keep them safe from accidents that may happen. Send angels to guard and protect them. In the name of the Father, the Son and the Holy Ghost, Amen, Amen, Amen, and Amen."

The prayer had to be exactly as it is written above. If she felt she skipped a word or confused the order, she had to re-state it in her mind. Charlotte felt that if she failed to say this prayer, it would result in something terrible happening to her family. She realized and acknowledged that God did not work this way, and that she was treating the prayer more like a superstition or magic phrase than a sincere prayer. However, the anxiety that she experienced if she failed to say the prayer was overwhelming. She shared that she probably had to say this prayer up to 150 times daily.

Finally, Jeff was a thirty-five-year-old man who described himself to me as a "committed Christian." Jeff was educated in private Christian schools and attended church regularly as an adult. He described having thoughts that he wasn't a good Christian because he felt he did not "pray enough." When asked to elaborate, Jeff told me that the Bible clearly indicates that "Christians are supposed to pray without ceasing." Discussions on what this passage of scripture referred to were not helpful to Jeff. He stated that he frequently notices that he is thinking about something "not spiritual" and then starts feeling "like a bad Christian because I should be praying." He responds to this obsessive thinking by praying over and over in his mind, "I love you Lord; thank you Lord; praise you Lord." This is usually said 3 times (once for the Father, Son, and Holy Spirit). Afterward, he feels better, at least until the obsessive thought returns and he repeats the ritual prayer. He even confided to me, "I've done it so many times now; it is getting a little insincere."

Undoing the Bad

Many Christians engage in religious rituals as part of the practice of their faith. Observing the Lord's supper is a well-known ritual for many Christians. Many Catholics observe the rituals of making the sign of the cross before and after prayer. Many Christian denominations observe baptism. These ritual behaviors are an important and healthy part of the practice of one's faith. However, there are times when these behaviors become compulsive and become part of the OCD symptom picture.

Sam was a sixteen-year-old high school junior who suffered from OCD. He had significant anxiety over anything he felt might be associated with evil or Satan. He feared entering music stores because he believed that many of the CD covers depicted "demonic images" and were "pure evil." He rarely watched television for fear that something "satanic" would come on and influence him. His fear of anything that he felt was "evil" was obsessive. Sam felt that he could protect himself from the "evilness" of these objects if he engaged in a ritual of crossing himself (head to navel followed by left to right shoulder) and tapping on his right thigh (since the left side represented bad and the right represented good) three times (once for each part of the Holy Trinity). Therefore, anytime he saw something that he felt represented evil, he would cross himself and tap his right thigh 3 times. He tried to do this subtly, but it was difficult to hide the crossing of himself when in public. His friends started to notice and ask questions. Sam did not feel that his friends would understand the real reason he was crossing himself. In fact, it seemed a little strange even to Sam. Usually, he made some excuse that did not satisfy his friends. They began to wonder about Sam, and eventually, his behavior began to have a negative effect on his social life.

Compulsive Scripture Quotation

When I was in college, I attended a church that taught the importance of memorizing scripture. The pastor also said that he felt it was a good idea to recite Bible verses aloud. He believed that one could memorize more effectively if one heard the verses aloud. He also believed that it was good to hear the Bible as often as possible. Memorizing and even saying aloud Bible verses is certainly not a pathological thing to do. However, reciting scripture can become a compulsive behavior for the Christian with OCD.

Gina was a twenty-five-year-old woman who attended a church that taught the value of learning scripture. In fact, Gina was quite an expert in the area of memorizing Bible verses. In some of the lighter moments of therapy with Gina, we would briefly play "stump the guest" which involved my trying to find a Bible verse that Gina could not finish from memory if she was read the first half. I don't think I was ever able to stump her. Gina also suffered from OCD. She felt that each time she had a thought that was impure, she needed to recite a Bible verse regarding that subject aloud. If she did, this would "erase" her impure thought and cleanse her from her sin. In addition to some faulty theology, Gina's compulsive recitation of scripture nearly cost her a very good job. Gina was a receptionist at a rather high-profile law firm. She was valued in her position because of her professional appearance, pleasant demeanor, good technical skills, and her excellent memory (which was obvious to all who knew of her memory for the Bible). Unfortunately, Gina often felt a compulsion to recite a verse of Scripture at inopportune times. Gina's desk was positioned such that the guests in the waiting room could see and hear her. Some rather high-profile clients began to raise questions that the receptionist was "walking around muttering about things." Gina realized that her behavior was not appropriate when she was on the job. However, her anxiety was too great to resist the compulsion to recite these verses.

Compulsive Confession

Confession of sin is a normal and healthy part of Christianity. For most Catholics, confession is more formal with the person confessing specific sins to his or her priest. For most Protestants, confession is equally important, but the confession of sin is more a direct prayer to God acknowledging one's sinfulness and need for forgiveness. It is my personal belief that the act of confession is God's method for man to *experience* God's forgiveness. There is something inherently healing about the act of acknowledging wrongdoing and feeling the relief of absolution. Theologically, forgiveness for the Christian is obtained through placing one's faith in Christ's death and resurrection as the sacrificial substitute for our sinfulness in order to obtain God's complete forgiveness. It is our faith in Christ's death and resurrection as sufficient payment for our sin that restores our relationship with God that was broken by man's sinful nature. As a Christian, confession of sin is God's method of helping us to remember that fact and to *experience* God's forgiveness rather than to *obtain* his forgiveness over and over. For many Christians suffering from OCD, the belief is that their forgiveness is dependent upon the confession of every individual sin on an ongoing basis. The fear is, "If I forget to confess one of them, I may not be forgiven and I will go to Hell when I die." This is an obsessional belief that is fueled by faulty theology.

Nevertheless, for the person with OCD, the anxiety caused by obsessive thoughts is independent of the lack of logic, truth, or rationality of obsessions. In response to the obsessive fear of going to Hell because of unconfessed sin, many Christians with OCD develop compulsive confessions. This may involve repeated trips to the confessional for the Catholic OCD sufferer. Marie was a forty-three-year-old married mother of five children. Her OCD symptoms included obsessive images of doing something violent to one of her children. Actually, Marie was viewed by all who knew her as the "perfect mother." Despite having three children ranging in age from 5 to 16 years, she managed to run her household in an organized and meticulous fashion. She was a good example of how someone with OCD can function at a very high level of competence and seem to the outside world to "have it all together." Her children were always well groomed and dressed in stylish clothes that looked as if they had just returned from a professional cleaner. They were well mannered and well behaved around other adults (even when parents were not present). Marie herself looked as though she had spent hours getting ready in the morning with hair, make-up and clothes all coordinated and stylish. Visitors to her home were amazed and often jealous of how she was able to keep everything in order. Even unannounced visitors could walk into Marie's house to find no dishes in the sink, no toys on the floor, and everything looking as though she had been expecting guests at any minute. Unfortunately, Marie was a tormented individual, but her turmoil was internal. Marie frequently talked about "my own private Hell" that existed in her mind. In

Chapter 1, I discussed aggressive obsessions that involve individuals being tormented by images of themselves engaging in aggressive or violent acts or by irrational fears that they may act in an aggressive or violent manner. Marie suffered from aggressive obsessions. She frequently had thoughts of slapping her children in the face. The fact is that she had never behaved aggressively toward any of her children in her 16 years of child rearing. Everyone who knew Marie described her as a patient, loving, and nurturing parent. Even her own teenage children described her as loving and patient. When a teenager describes a parent as patient and fair, no further proof is needed! Despite the reality of Marie's gentle nature and loving behavior toward her children, the obsessions continued. In addition to the images of slapping her children, Marie also had more disturbing images that flashed through her mind including images of her stabbing them with knives or throwing boiling water on them. The anxiety caused by these images and thoughts was overwhelming for Marie. In therapy with Marie, she acknowledged that she sometimes became frustrated with her children (as all parents do), but she never behaved in an inappropriate manner.

Marie was a deeply religious and devout Catholic who believed that she had sinned each time she had an image of behaving violently toward her children. She made frequent trips to the confessional in order to confess her "sinful thoughts" and to obtain forgiveness. Since she attended a small church, she found herself making confessions to the same priest often. At first, Marie confessed her images weekly. However, as her obsessions worsened, she found herself making daily trips to the confessional. Father John was a young priest with no experience and little understanding in the area of OCD. He did not recognize her thoughts as a symptom of OCD and was rather disturbed upon hearing Marie share with him, "I saw myself taking Mary Grace (her 5-year-old daughter) by the head and twisting it around until her neck snapped and her body fell lifeless in my arms." Father John heard about several of these types of images in detail. Marie also shared how she saw herself "take a hammer and beat Andrew (her 12-year-old son) in the face until all of his teeth fell out into the floor." Father John began to worry that Marie may be dangerous. He felt that her thoughts might be symptomatic of a problem with anger and worried that she might harm her children. He suggested that she might suffer from a serious problem and recommended that she get help. At first, Marie was devastated and felt that this was confirmation that she was a bad and evil person. She became depressed and even had suicidal thoughts. Fortunately, her condition was properly diagnosed and treated.

Jimmy was a ten-year-old boy who was raised in a good Christian home with parents who loved him very much. Jimmy was taught from an early age that "if you confess your sins to Jesus, he will forgive you." Jimmy was a conscientious young boy who sincerely wanted to do the right thing. From a young age, he prayed with his parents each and every night before bed for God to forgive him for his sins. At first, he listed things like "being mean to my brother" and "sneaking a cookie when I wasn't supposed to." However, his parents noticed that his "sin list" was growing. He started to ask for forgiveness for things such as, "not asking the girl who was crying in church if she was OK." Keep in mind, Jimmy did not know the girl in church who was crying. He also added things like, "seeing litter on the playground and not throwing it in the trash can." His list of things he felt he needed to confess grew to the point that his bedtime prayer could take literally 2 hours each night. He then found that the list of things grew to the point that he couldn't possibly remember all of them throughout the day, so he had to "confess" to his parents several times throughout the day. His parents were perplexed by this behavior. On the one hand, they were glad that Jimmy seemed to be such a moral young boy who wanted to please God. On the other hand, they knew that something was wrong, and Jimmy seemed miserable.

Magical Prevention

As we discussed earlier, a frequent OCD symptom includes an obsessive fear that the person will act out impulsively and inappropriately. For the Christian with OCD, this often translates into a fear of impulsive sinful behavior. These thoughts and fears torment individuals, despite no history of ever acting in a way they fear they might. Some patients develop religious compulsive behaviors that are believed to prevent them from acting impulsively.

Mike was a twenty-three-year-old who had been dating a girl in his church for eight months. Both he and his girlfriend shared the commitment of not making their relationship sexual until after they married. They did all the right things to make sure that they did not make it more difficult for them to keep this commitment. As expected, Mike was struggling with some normal temptation. I talked openly with Mike about his struggle being a normal one. I reinforced his decision to wait until after marriage before making the relationship sexual and told him that there were many advantages to doing so. I shared with him that it was good that he found his girlfriend attractive, and that it was normal to have feelings that made him want to become more physical with her. However, Mike did not accept his feelings as normal. In fact, he developed an obsessive thought or fear that he would uncontrollably force his girlfriend into a sexual encounter. He developed a behavior that he believed may prevent him from becoming a sexual aggressor. Mike clung to the scripture verse 1 Corinthians 6:18 (*NIV*) that reads, "Flee from sexual immorality. All other sins a man commits are outside his body, but he who sins sexually sins against his own body." Mike then felt the need to trace the word "flee" on his thigh several times. He felt that this would prevent him from acting on his impulses. Unfortunately, the behavior needed to be repeated almost as often as he felt attracted to his girlfriend. He began constantly tracing the word "flee" on his thigh to the point that he was developing an irritation on his skin from constant tracing. The entire experience became so painful for George he began to avoid his girlfriend. As with most people with OCD, George did not tell her the real reason he was avoiding her for fear that either she would not understand, or that she would think he was "crazy." Needless to say, his girlfriend interpreted his avoidance as an indication that he was losing interest in her. Consequently, she began to withdraw her feelings in an effort to protect herself emotionally. George's case is a good example of how OCD can affect relationships and those individuals close to the person suffering with the disorder. The symptoms of OCD are confusing to loved ones of those affected by this disease. Often the person with OCD is ashamed of their symptoms or feels he cannot explain the thoughts or behaviors. Therefore, they often try to hide or mask the symptoms which can lead to avoidance.

Conclusion

OCD is a non-discriminatory illness. It affects people of all ages, genders, and religions. For the Christian with OCD, the symptoms of OCD often incorporate the beliefs and behaviors associated with the person's spiritual life. This is particularly true for those Christians to whom their faith is an important part of their life. Some people erroneously believe that this means that OCD is a "spiritual problem" instead of a psychiatric condition. This conclusion can lead to confusion and harmful recommendations within the Christian community. It is vital that the church understand what OCD is and how people suffering from OCD can receive proper diagnosis and treatment for their condition.

SIX

The Obsessive-Compulsive Spectrum and Co-morbid Disorders

While OCD is a disorder that lends itself to specific definition and description, real life is much more complex. Some individuals experience specific OCD symptoms that can be clearly observed and manifest exactly as described in textbooks. Just as often, however, individuals have symptoms of OCD along with other symptoms that do not fit the classic definition of OCD.

In his book, *Obsessive-Compulsive Disorders: A Complete Guide to Getting Well and Staying Well*, Fred Penzel, Ph.D. describes the "OC Spectrum" as a family or spectrum of disorders that seem to be related to OCD like members of an extended family. The OC Spectrum includes: Body Dysmorphic Disorder (BDD); Trichotillomania (TTM); compulsive skin picking and nail biting; and Tourette's Disorder (TD). While each of these disorders has separate symptoms that distinguish one from another, they share the following common characteristics according to Dr. Penzel: 1) the individuals find their symptoms repetitive and intrusive; 2) individuals attempt to resist the symptoms; 3) individuals feel anxious because of the symptoms of these disorders; and 4) the individuals experience a disruption in their lives because of the disorder.[1]

There appears to be a higher rate of these disorders among individuals with OCD. For example:

- studies have found rates ranging from 15 to 37 percent of BDD among individuals with OCD
- studies have indicated approximately 20 percent (1 in 5) of OCD patients meet criteria for Tourette's Disorder (the rate of TD in the general population is about 1 in 100 boys and 1 in 600 girls)
- studies have found between 36 and 68 percent of TD patients also have OCD
- studies have shown between 13 and 27 percent of TTM patients also had OCD
- a study showed 23 percent of OCD patients engaged in skin picking as opposed to 7 percent of a non-OCD sample

I will offer a brief description of these disorders in order to help the reader understand the differences between them.

Body Dysmorphic Disorder (BDD)

BDD is a disorder diagnosed when a person develops a pre-occupation with what they believe to be a defect in the way they look. Patients with BDD become focused on a slight or imagined defect in their physical appearance. They may become preoccupied by the belief that an aspect of their body is asymmetrical; that a body part is too large or too small; that a certain aspect of their body is misshapen; etc. There is no specific aspect of appearance on which patients with BDD might focus. In fact, patients with BDD may change the focus of their distress over time. For example, a patient with BDD may be preoccupied by the belief that one eye is larger than another for a period of time. Later, the same person may become obsessed with the belief that their ears are deformed because they are "too pointy." BDD patients are not individuals who have difficulty accepting real disfigurations or deformities. Rather, they are individuals who would be judged by most people as "perfectly normal." However, they are convinced that they have a significant abnormality in their physical appearance. Most patients with BDD suffer significant social impairment due to their embarrassment and self-consciousness. In fact, some individuals with BDD become housebound. Additionally, many BDD patients suffer from depression. Some patients with BDD actually pursue plastic surgery as an option for their dissatisfaction of their appearance. The majority of BDD patients develop compulsions including checking their appearance in a mirror; masking or hiding their imagined flaws; and seeking reassurance.

Trichotillomania (TTM)

Trichotillomania is a disorder that involves the recurrent pulling out of one's hair, resulting in noticeable hair loss. This typically begins in childhood with onset beginning around age 5 to 8 years. In some cases, children may show transient periods of hair pulling that stop with no intervention. However, some individuals experience hair pulling into adulthood. For some, hair pulling is continuous, while for others it may be episodic (e.g., symptoms may come and go for weeks, months, or years at a time).

Patients with TTM may pull hair from a variety of areas including hair from the head; eyelashes; eyebrows; the pubic area; underarms; etc. Patients with TTM often pull hair during episodes throughout the day. For some TTM patients, hair pulling is at times automatic. In fact, some of these individuals have little or no awareness that they are pulling out their hair. For some TTM patients, they report a pleasurable or soothing feeling when pulling their hair. For almost all TTM patients, there is a feeling of distress over their hair pulling and over the fact that they cannot seem to stop the behavior.

Some individuals with TTM actually swallow the hair after they pull it. When this is done excessively, there is a risk that the individual may develop a trichobezoar, which is a hairball that can block the intestinal tract. In some cases, surgery is needed to correct this problem.

TTM usually results in the development of bald spots or thinning spots in the areas from which hair is pulled. I have worked with many patients with TTM. Some have pulled bald or thinning spots from the crown of the scalp. Others have pulled hair from the front of the scalp. Still others have pulled hair from the side of the head, directly above the ears. I have worked with TTM patients who have pulled out every eyelash, and others who have plucked out their eyebrows. When TTM patients pull from their head, they often attempt to hide the bald or thinning spot if possible. This is easier for females, or for males with longer hair who can simply let their hair cover a specific spot. One teenage girl I worked with had long hair. I never saw her wear her hair in any manner other than pulled back. I knew that she suffered from TTM and that she pulled hair from the side of her head. She informed me that when her hair was down, the thinning hair around the side of her head was noticeable. However, when pulled back, no one could see the thinning spots on her head. Other individuals with TTM frequently wear hats or bandanas to cover bald or thinning spots. Obviously, it is impossible to hide or mask the absence of eyelashes and eyebrows.

Patients with TTM suffer significant embarrassment from the results of their symptoms. They often avoid everyday activities like going to a barber or hairdresser. They also may avoid activities like swimming which may highlight their hair loss. Many TTM patients find their disorder to cause social distress. For parents, having a child with TTM can be extremely anxiety producing. In my clinical experience, TTM in children can cause parents significant distress. Most parents have no idea that such a disorder exists, and the symptoms can be baffling and frightening. Many parents resort to punishment and shaming in attempts to get their children to stop pulling their hair out. Unfortunately, these methods are ineffective at best, and can actually increase the symptoms.

Fortunately, TTM patients respond to treatment including habit reversal training and/or medication. I will be discussing medication for OCD in chapter 8. There I will list some medications commonly used to treat OCD. Due to the correlations between the origins of these disorders, some medications commonly used to treat OCD are efficacious for treating TTM as well. For a specific description of habit reversal training to treat TTM, Dr. Penzel describes in detail a self-help program for treating TTM in his book *Obsessive-Compulsive Disorders: A Complete Guide to Getting Well and Staying Well*, pages 86-111.

Tourette's Disorder (TD)

The *Diagnostic and Statistical Manual for Mental Disorder—Fourth Edition (DSM-IV)* defines Tourette's Disorder as the presence of multiple motor tics and one or more vocal tic which occur many times daily nearly every day for a period of more than 1 year. A tic is defined as a sudden, rapid, recurrent, stereotyped motor movement or vocalization. Tics are experienced by individuals as irresistible; however, they can be suppressed for some time. Tics take many forms. A partial list of tics includes:

Motor tics
- eye blinking*
- eye rolling/squinting
- finger tapping
- head jerking/rolling*
- nose twitching
- eye twitching
- facial grimacing
- hand clenching/unclenching
- jaw/mouth moving
- joint cracking
- jumping
- hopping
- leg jerking
- lip licking/smacking
- muscle flexing/unflexing
- shoulder shrugging/rolling*
- teeth clenching/unclenching
- tongue thrusting

(* indicates the most commonly seen motor tics)

Motor tics can be simple (i.e., involving one movement or gesture) or complex (i.e., involving a series of movements or gestures).

Vocal Tics
- barking
- belching
- coughing
- throat clearing*
- sniffing*
- grunting
- humming
- making animal noises
- making "tsk," or "pft" noises
- making guttural sounds
- screeching
- shouting
- calling out
- making "hmm," "oh," "wow," "uh" noises
- snorting
- moaning
- blowing noises
- shrieking
- whistling

(* indicates the most commonly seen vocal tics)

Vocal tics can also be simple (i.e., one sound) or complex (i.e., a series of sounds). Complex vocal tics can include repeating words or phrases out of context and may include palilalia (repeating one's own sounds or words) or echolalia (repeating the last heard word, sound, or phrase).

Tourette's is often overlooked in clinical practice because of inaccurate stereotypes of how the disorder manifests. Television shows frequently portray people with TD as individuals who spontaneously shout or utter profanities. This symptom is known as copralalia and can be one of many vocal tics. However, the majority of TD patients do not manifest this symptom. In fact, only about 10 to 15 percent of TD patients develop copralalia. Many individuals with TD manifest subtle tics that are difficult to recognize, or are often "explained away" as being caused by something else. For example, children with a sniffing or throat clearing tic are often believed to suffer chronic allergy and/or sinus problems. It is important to differentiate symptoms caused by actual physiological problems versus a tic when these symptoms are present.

The average age of onset of TD is 6.5 years. Over one-half of diagnoses of TD are made because another individual or family member affected by TD recognized the symptoms in the individual. TD is considered a chronic, lifelong disorder. The course of this disorder varies among individuals. It is estimated that 30 to 40 percent of TD patients have symptoms that disappear by late adolescence; 30 percent have symptoms that decrease by late adolescence; and 50 percent have symptoms that persist into adulthood. As mentioned earlier, tics can be suppressed for varying periods of time. However, they cannot be suppressed indefinitely. A common experience is that of a school-aged child who is able to successfully suppress tics for the majority of the school day only to find that the tics are worse at home. It is almost as if they have been "stored up" and are released at home. Tics wax and wane over the course of time. Stress clearly exacerbates tics. Tics can also change over the course of time. It is not unusual for a person to experience a specific motor or vocal tic for a period of time only to find that the tic "disappears" but is replaced later by a different motor or vocal tic.

In her book *Teaching the Tiger: A Handbook for Individuals Involved in the Education of Students with Attention Deficit Disorders, Tourette Syndrome or Obsessive-Compulsive Disorder,* Marilyn Dornbush, Ph.D., and Sheryl K. Pruitt, M.Ed., describe the concept of a *storm.* Sheryl Pruitt developed the term to describe the behavioral "meltdown" that can occur with TD patients. She states that TD patients can become overaroused in stressful situations which results in a temporary impairment in problem-solving abilities. She states that during these episodes, a person has limited access to abstract knowledge and impaired ability to comprehend and sequence the consequences of inappropriate and abusive attitudes, actions and verbalizations. Sensory input increases the storm and leads to a more violent outburst. She states that when the *storm* subsides, the individual is typically remorseful and surprised by the behavior.[2]

At present, there is no cure for TD. Patients with TD learn to effectively manage stress which can exacerbate tics. In addition, TD patients may benefit from therapy designed to help them with associated difficulties such as self-esteem problems; depression; social or interpersonal difficulties; and learning to live with the disorder.

Skin Picking and Nail Biting
While BDD, TTM, and TD are all disorders listed in the *DSM-IV,* skin picking and nail biting are not. However, Dr. Penzel

has listed this condition as part of the OC Spectrum. He makes a clear distinction between "normal" nail biting or picking at the skin and the point at which it becomes a "disorder." The technical terms are onychophagia for compulsive nail biting and neurotic excoriation for compulsive skin picking. He describes compulsive skin picking as picking to the point of creating open sores and then picking at the scabs that result. He also includes squeezing and digging at pimples and blackheads with fingers or other implements to the point of causing infections and scarring of the tissue. He defines compulsive nail biting as biting the nails to the point of bleeding and disfigured fingertips. Infections are often the result.

I worked with a young man who was diagnosed with OCD. He was a young man in his mid-20's who met classic diagnostic criteria for OCD. He also suffered from compulsive skin picking. He always had a sore on his face about which he was obviously self-conscious. He frequently arrived to our sessions at least 30 minutes late, and apologized for being tardy, typically blaming the traffic. Because traffic in Atlanta can be brutal, it is not unusual for people to arrive late to appointments during peak traffic times. However, after arriving late for several consecutive sessions that were scheduled during midday, I confronted him by saying, "You know, Glen, there usually isn't much traffic at 11:00 A.M. Is that really why you were late today?" He seemed embarrassed and told me that the real reason he had been late for every appointment was that he would normally pull into the parking lot of the office in plenty of time to make the appointment. However, he felt he had to check his face in the rearview mirror of his car just before getting out. This would inevitably result in him finding a blemish that he felt he had to pick. He described being unable to stop picking, despite the fact that he would usually pick until he started bleeding. Afterward, he would have to go into the bathroom to clean his face and hands and to stop the bleeding. This example illustrates several characteristics associated with compulsive skin picking. First, the patient is often embarrassed by the behavior. They often hide the behavior from others. Second, patients affected by compulsive skin picking spend inordinate amounts of time involved in the behavior. Third, the behavior causes them great distress and frequently physical harm. Finally, the behavior is experienced by the patient as being out of control. The patient is simply unable to stop on his or her own, despite negative consequences.

Comorbid Disorders

The disorders included in the OC Spectrum are believed to be related to one another both in terms of the types of symptoms as well as in their genetic association. However, there are other disorders that frequently occur along with OCD. Although these disorders are not believed to be linked genetically to OCD, they are frequently seen clinically as *co-morbid* disorders. The term co-morbid indicates that the disorder occurs *along with* another disorder. Several disorders are frequently seen as co-morbid to OCD including depression, substance abuse problems, and attention-deficit hyperactivity disorder (ADHD). Many books have been written on each of these disorders, and some resources listed at the end of this book might be helpful for anyone dealing with co-morbid disorders. I discussed depression, ADHD, and substance abuse with children and teenagers in Chapter 4. These same issues apply to adults.

Another co-morbid feature for some patients with OCD is the presence of panic attacks. According to the *DSM-IV*, a panic attack is an intense and sudden onset of fear or discomfort in which 4 or more of the following symptoms develop acutely:

- palpitations, pounding heart or accelerated heart rate
- sweating
- trembling or shaking
- sensations of shortness of breath or smothering
- feeling of choking
- chest pain or discomfort
- nausea or abdominal distress
- feeling dizzy, unsteady, lightheaded, or faint
- derealization (feelings of unreality) or depersonalization (being detached from oneself)
- fear of losing control or going crazy
- fear of dying
- paresthesias (numbness or tingling sensations)
- chills or hot flashes

A panic attack is not, in and of itself, a specific disorder. Rather, several anxiety disorders may include the symptom of panic attacks. It is important to understand what a panic attack is, and that it can occur in patients with OCD since panic attacks are often misunderstood. Usually, when a person has a panic attack for the first time, they have no idea what is happening to them. In fact, many people who experience panic attacks mistakenly believe that they may be having a heart attack. This is because many of the symptoms of a panic attack mimic those of a cardiac arrest (e.g., racing heart; tightness in chest; shortness of breath; sweating; etc.). A common scenario is one in which a person has a panic attack and ends up in an emergency room of a hospital fearing that they are dying. These people often leave dismayed after being told by the emergency room physician that their symptoms are caused by "stress." Panic attacks are incredibly frightening to the individual. In many cases, if a person has a panic attack, they develop *anticipatory anxiety* which refers to persistent worry and concern that they may have another panic attack.

It is typical for a person who has a panic attack to try to determine what caused the panic attack. This results in the person replaying every event that occurred just prior to the attack in an effort to figure out what caused it. Many times, the person experienced an unexpected panic attack (one which occurs in the absence of a situational precipitant). The person may erroneously attribute something that happened to the panic attack and subsequently avoid any contact with that object, person, or situation. For example, I worked with Morris who had an unexpected panic attack in a movie theater. There was nothing particularly disturbing or even unusual about the movie or any other aspect of the situation when Morris had the panic attack. However, because the experience was so terrifying to him, he was determined to discover what caused it. He reasoned that if he could find the "thing" that caused his panic attack, he could successfully avoid it and consequently avoid any future panic attacks. Unfortunately, his panic attack was not "caused" by any aspect of the situation. Morris initially avoided movies, certain that it was the darkened theater and something about the movie itself that caused it. After experiencing a second panic attack nowhere near a theater, he correctly deduced that movies were not the prime suspect. He then tried to find the common elements associated with the two panic attacks. He somehow determined that he was too warm each time. Therefore, he made it his mission to never allow himself to become too warm. Unfortunately for Morris, he had a third panic attack at a time when he was quite chilly. This detective work went on for several panic attacks, with Morris avoiding crowds, certain types of fragrances, eating certain types of foods, and even being around certain people. Finally, he realized that there was no obvious cause for his panic attack.

It should be noted that some people have panic attacks that *are* precipitated by certain stimuli. In the case of phobias, for example, some people find that their panic attacks are precipitated by exposure to certain stimuli. In my clinical experience, unexpected panic attacks are more common.

Panic attacks, like so many anxiety disorders, run in families. They are clearly believed to be caused by physiological factors and can be effectively treated with medication and/or therapy. I believe that it is important to understand what a panic attack is when attempting to understand OCD since panic attacks can co-occur and are often a source of fear and confusion among patients.

The purpose of this chapter is to educate the reader about the clinical complexity of OCD. OCD is a disorder that is believed to be associated genetically with several other disorders. Additionally, there are several disorders that are frequently seen as co-existing with OCD. The following diagram illustrates how symptoms of various disorders can overlap with one another:

Clinical Complexity

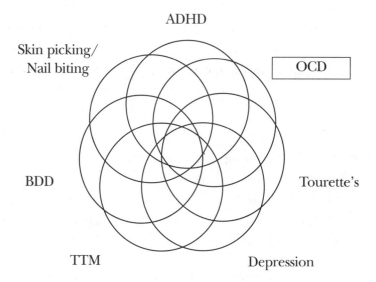

Without some understanding of these disorders, it is easy to become confused by symptoms that do not fit the traditional definition of OCD. Making an accurate *differential diagnosis* (understanding which disorders may be causing which symptoms) is essential for proper treatment planning. A competent professional may be helpful in making an accurate differential diagnosis for individuals experiencing a variety of symptoms.

SEVEN

Treating OCD with Non-Pharmacological Interventions

The good news for patients with OCD is that it is a treatable disorder. Treatment outcome research for OCD demonstrates high success rates using non-pharmacological treatment (not using medicine) methods alone. In the next chapter, I will discuss the uses of medication for treating OCD. However, many people achieve substantial improvement utilizing treatments without medication. In fact, studies have shown improvement rates up to 90 percent for patients who complete treatment. Non-pharmacological treatment approaches generally fall into two categories: behavior therapy and cognitive therapy.

Behavior Therapy

Behavior therapy is based largely on the principles of learning theory. Behavior therapists believe that most human behavior is learned. Consequently, behavior that one wants to change can be *un-learned*. Behavior therapy involves teaching people how to make specific modifications to their actual behavior in order to stop maladaptive patterns of reacting and to learn new, healthier, and more adaptive ways of responding.

Cognitive Therapy

Cognitive Therapy is based on the theory that humans react to things (both emotionally as well as behaviorally) based upon how they *think* about the thing they are responding to. Cognitive therapy involves teaching people to identify irrational, illogical, or unhealthy beliefs that they have about the things in their lives in order to modify or change these beliefs into ones that are more rational, logical, and healthy.

Two Is Better Than One

In treating OCD, many professionals find techniques from both of these approaches to be extremely helpful in treating OCD. The term cognitive-behavior therapy (CBT) is one that implies the use of both behavioral and cognitive therapy approaches in treating a particular disorder. Most therapists who treat OCD use techniques from CBT to treat OCD. Most controlled studies that measure outcome of OCD treatment use a very specific technique in order to assess the treatment efficacy of a particular technique or component of therapy. However, most professionals in clinical practice use an approach that they feel comfortable using and that they feel will be effective for the particular patient they are treating. Good clinicians understand that even the best treatment technique may need to be modified some to accommodate a particular individual. Because individuals are so unique, seasoned clinicians understand that simply applying a technique without regard for the individual is not the best approach. I have developed an approach for treating OCD that is based on empirically validated cognitive-behavioral approaches. Some of my approach is not at all unique and is based on what has been shown for years to be effective in treating OCD. However, I have developed some interventions that are my own creation simply because patients have indicated that they found these particular interventions helpful.

The Treatment

Education

Before starting any intervention for an individual with OCD, it is imperative that the person understand what OCD is *and* what OCD is *not*. Hopefully, the earlier chapters of this book will help individuals better understand that OCD is a biological disorder that has nothing to do with one's spiritual condition, moral character, childhood issues, etc. It is also my hope that the earlier chapters will help individuals to recognize obsessions and compulsions. Most patients that I have worked with did not always know that some of their "crazy thoughts" were actually obsessions or that their behaviors were compulsions. In order to treat OCD, one must be able to recognize how it is manifesting.

When I begin working with someone who has OCD, I make certain that they *externalize* OCD. In other words, they need to see OCD as a disorder that is separate from them. For older adolescents and adults, simply referring to it as OCD (assuming both they and I are referring to the same thing) is enough. For younger children, a more tangible metaphor or analogy may be necessary. For instance, I talk about "the OCD part of your brain that tells you to worry and do those silly habits" to help them realize that OCD is not *them*. For children who suffer from frequent obsessions, I talk about the "worry facto-ry" and help them envision a part of their brain that works overtime to make "worry thoughts." For older children and adolescents, I ask them to think about OCD as a heckler at a baseball game. Most of us have had the experience of attend-ing a baseball game and seeing a heckler in the stands shout-ing insults at the batter in an effort to distract the batter. He may shout things like, "Hey, this guy can't hit anything" or "OK pitcher, this is an automatic strike out." I also discuss thinking of obsessive thoughts and worries as junk mail or spam e-mail. We all have had the experience of receiving mail from someone who does not know us. I tell my patients that I get junk mail and spam e-mail every day. I didn't ask for it, and the people who send it to me do not even know who I am. Most of the time, the junk mail is an effort to get me to buy something that I neither need nor want. I explain that I usu-ally throw the junk mail away and delete the spam e-mail with-out even opening it since it is usually just a waste of my time to read it anyway. I explain that obsessive thoughts are really the same thing. I explain that in OCD, these thoughts are sent randomly to try and get you to "buy into worrying" and to get you to do some compulsive behavior that costs time and ener-gy. These analogies help the person to understand that OCD is a foreign entity—not part of them. This makes it easier to follow through with the treatment we will discuss later.

Educating patients about OCD is not a one-session event. This is an ongoing part of the treatment process. Many patients become good at recognizing their obsessive thoughts and compulsive acts. However, OCD will frequently sneak in an obsessive thought that "gets by" the new awareness of the patient. At these times, it is important to point out that "this sounds like one of those OCD thoughts to me. . . what do you think?" I recall one patient who became her own expert on OCD. She became invested in her own therapy and dedicated herself to learning as much as she could about her disorder. After a few months of treatment, I was convinced that she could teach a college level class on OCD. Her OCD symptoms were under control, and she had become superb at using the techniques she learned. In a routine follow-up visit, she began to tell me about her new boyfriend. I noticed that she was describing excessive concerns about things she said to him. She seemed to be worrying about specific words she used and how he might interpret her. I listened for a few minutes and then remarked, "You know, Sarah, I might be wrong, but it sounds like you are obsessing a bit here. Any chance some of your worries are coming from OCD?" She tilted her head slightly, paused, and then said, "You know, you are absolutely right! I didn't even see it, but that's exactly what I'm doing." This insight helped Sarah stop devoting useless time and energy to these obsessive thoughts. As we said earlier, OCD symptoms can change over time. It is important to help patients understand that even after you kick Mr. OCD out, he may try to sneak back into the party disguised in a different outfit.

Part of the pre-treatment education involves not only identifying the enemy (OCD), but also preparing for battle. I tell my patients that OCD is stubborn. I usually say something like, "He does not raise the white flag and surrender just because we have blown his cover and exposed him for who he is. He is going to put up a considerable effort to stay camped right there in your brain trying to make your life miserable. We can beat him and drive him out, but I want you to be ready for a fight." For Christians, I point out that the Bible is full of stories where God led his people into battle, even against overwhelming odds, only to give them victory. I tell them, "OCD may look like Goliath right now, but just like God helped David slay a giant, I have no doubt that he will help you beat OCD. In fact, the more you understand about OCD, the less gigantic he will seem to you." I tell people that it's not only acceptable, but even helpful to allow themselves to become angry at OCD. As we will discuss later, some of the active phases of treatment for OCD result in temporary increases in anxiety levels for brief periods of time. Getting angry at OCD can actually help patients deal with the anxiety more effectively. There is a term known as *reciprocal inhibition* which means that it is difficult for a person to experience two incompatible emotions at the same time. For example, it is unlikely that you can feel fearful and relaxed at the same time. One will cancel out the other. In a similar way, anger and anxiety seem to compete for the same space. Many people tell me that when they are angry, they are not conscious of being anxious or afraid. It is sometimes helpful when combating OCD to get mad at it in order to persevere in the fight against it.

Another important part of education for patients with OCD is to help them establish goals for their treatment. I ask my patients to envision what their life would be like if they did not have OCD. I want them to think about specific things they would do that they have difficulty doing now. I want them to think about things they would not avoid or have anxiety around. I encourage them to think about how they would behave differently if they didn't worry so much about the things they worry about now. I believe that this is important because by the time a patient comes to me and is correctly diagnosed, they have probably been suffering from OCD for a long time. Remember that the average person spends about 9 years before receiving a correct diagnosis for OCD. Most patients I have spoken with tell me that before receiving treatment for OCD, they "tried everything" to overcome their disorder. Many of these people simply gave up and resigned themselves to a life of "worry and weirdness" after their efforts to stop their symptoms failed. For many of these patients, they have trouble seeing their life free from OCD symptoms. Because the treatment is not always easy, I believe that it is important for people to have a vision of what they can accomplish in order to help maintain the motivation to persevere through some of the "work" of treatment.

I have found that some patients are resistant to treatment due to their *dichotomous thinking* about the outcome. Dichotomous thinking refers to the tendency to see the world in terms of one extreme or the other. In the case of OCD, I have encountered many individuals who find some of their OCD tendencies adaptive. For example, they describe their punctuality, orderliness, and attention to small details as aspects of their functioning that are valued. They mistakenly see these as part and parcel of their disorder and believe that if treatment does free them from OCD, they will move to the opposite end of the continuum of these traits. For example, they fear that instead of being obsessively punctual, compulsively organized, and perfectionistic, successful treatment will transform them into an individual who is chronically late, hopelessly disorganized, and laissez-faire or careless about everything. It is important to remind these individuals that virtually all characteristics of human functioning exist on a continuum. I often draw a continuum for such an individual that looks something like this:

OCD ———————————————————— Anti-OCD

"The Zone"

Using this continuum, I explain that the OCD end of the continuum is that area that includes all of their OCD symptoms including all of the obsessive thoughts and worries and compulsive behaviors that currently cause them such misery. The Anti-OCD end of the continuum includes the opposite of the traits we think of as obsessive and compulsive. For example, a person on this end of the continuum may be described as not caring about any details, rules, etc. This end of the continuum includes such traits as disorganization; carelessness; tardiness; lack of scruples; messiness; etc. The fear for many OCD patients is that if they let go of the OCD end of the continuum, they will automatically swing to the other end. This, of course, would be unacceptable to most people with OCD. I point out that it is perfectly acceptable to live a healthy and happy life closer to the OCD end of the continuum, as long as they are not on the extreme end. I explain that it is even fine to be closer to the OCD end than to the middle. Many high-functioning people show a tendency toward obsessiveness or compulsiveness, but do not suffer from OCD. I call this area "the zone" and indicate that the goal of treatment can be to eliminate or reduce the OCD symptoms without decreasing their effectiveness or productivity. In fact, by eliminating or reducing the OCD symptoms and staying in "the zone," they will actually become *more* effective and productive.

Predicting the course of treatment is also part of education. Treatment for OCD is not always pleasant and fun. I find it extremely important to try to maintain a sense of humor about OCD and to help patients learn to laugh at their own disorder in order to keep a perspective. However, there are phases of treatment when patients will not be laughing. The most essential component of the non-pharmacological treatment for OCD is exposure and response prevention (which I will fully explain later). This phase of treatment will require the patient to tolerate a temporary increase in anxiety levels. I tell patients up front that the treatment approach I use includes techniques that are proven to be effective, but that they will sometimes be difficult to do. I explain that at times they will probably get mad at me for asking them to do things that make them more anxious since they came to see me in order to feel less anxious. I explain that they will undoubtedly say at some point, "Some of these things you want me to do are harder than having OCD. Sometimes I think it would be easier to just learn to live with the OCD than to do these things." I tell them that these thoughts and feelings are normal and to expect them. I also tell them that treatment for OCD is a lot like the physical therapy I had to undergo for a shoulder injury: that there were many times when the rehabilitation was much more painful than the injury itself, but that my shoulder would never have improved without the therapy and that the pain was worth it. I tell them that if they push through the hard part of the therapy, there is a 90 percent chance that they will see a substantial improvement in their OCD. Predicting this for patients is important because many patients have second thoughts about treatment at some point.

Exposure and Response Prevention

Current research indicates that the most effective form of non-pharmacological treatment for OCD is Exposure and Response Prevention (E/RP). This method of treatment consists of a therapist and patient cooperating together to gradually expose the patient to anxiety-provoking obsessive thoughts while resisting the urge to engage in the compulsive behaviors that serve to decrease the anxiety that follows the obsessive thoughts. When done correctly, this form of treatment is highly effective in reducing obsessive thoughts and compulsive behaviors, and the improvement lasts over time.

The initial phase of this approach requires the patient to "rank" anxiety-producing situations (those that elicit obsessive thoughts) from least to most severe. It is usually helpful to ask the patient to assign a number value from 1 to 100 with 1 being a non-anxiety situation and 100 being the worst type of anxiety possible. This is helpful for both the patient and the therapist to communicate with each other about anxiety-producing situations.

Next, the therapist explains that in order to overcome OCD, there is really no other method that will work than to confront each situation and to overcome it. Most patients at this point become anxious and tell the therapist, "You don't understand, I've already tried that and it doesn't work." The therapist calmly informs the patient the previous efforts have been unsuccessful because the patient did not have the proper tools and did not use the appropriate method to beat OCD. I use an analogy to illustrate the point. I explain that trying to beat OCD without any professional help is like trying to play a football game using the wrong players in the wrong positions. Imagine putting your quarterback at offensive tackle; your center at wide receiver; etc. Besides looking pretty silly, you would certainly lose the game. I explain that I will act as their coach and help them put the right players in the right positions using a strategy that will certainly work for them.

The technique of E/RP is relatively simple, but wonderfully effective. The patient starts out by resisting the typical compulsive behavior associated with their least anxiety-producing situation. I use the diagram below to illustrate how it works:

Response Prevention

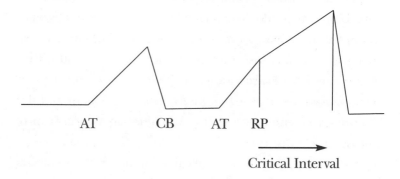

In the above diagram, the x-axis represents the passage of time while the y-axis represents anxiety levels from low to high. AT refers to an "anxiety thought." This is any situation that results in any type of obsessive doubt, worry, thought, image, etc., which begins to raise anxiety. CB represents any type of compulsive behavior (e.g., washing, checking, compulsive praying; etc.). As the diagram shows, performing a compulsive behavior immediately results in a reduction of anxiety to the same level as before the anxiety thought occurred. Prior to treatment, this pattern would continue ad infinitum. The patient may have different anxiety-producing thoughts and perform different compulsive behaviors. However, the pattern would continue in the same predictable way. On the diagram above, the second AT still refers to an anxiety-producing thought. However, in this example, at the point the patient would previously perform a compulsive behavior (CB), I ask them to resist the compulsive behavior (Response Prevention or RP). At this point, you see that the anxiety level actually increases beyond the point the patient normally allows anxiety to rise. It is important to predict this rise in anxiety and to explain that this is to be anticipated. The graph also shows that if the patient continues to resist the urge to perform the compulsive behavior, their anxiety level will ultimately decrease spontaneously and will return to the normal level without having to perform a compulsive behavior. I have labeled the time from the moment the patient resists the compulsion (RP) to the time when the anxiety level falls as the *critical interval.* This is the interval of time that *must be endured* in order to break the pattern of OCD. Without fail, most patients who attempt to do this on their own are unable to endure the critical interval. Many patients erroneously believe that their anxiety may continue to rise to an intolerable level, or that their anxiety will never decrease unless they perform the compulsive behavior. Most patients who successfully endure the critical interval tell me that it normally takes only about 20 to

30 minutes before their anxiety begins to fall. This may sound like a brief time, but for the patient with OCD, it can seem like an eternity. This is particularly true if the fear is that their anxiety may never stop. I have found that it is much easier to make it through the critical interval if the patient has something to distract him during this time. I often instruct the patient to have something else that they can get involved in to help them not to sit and dwell on the fact that they are anxious. If a patient can make it through a critical interval without performing a compulsive behavior, it is a great success which should be celebrated. Each time a patient is successful with E/RP, he is in fact weakening the grip of OCD on his life.

Tools for the Critical Interval

There are several things that a person can do during the critical interval to increase their ability to resist the compulsive behavior. Let me offer a few that have worked for my patients:

1. Memorize scripture.
   - Every Christian has his or her own favorite passages of Scripture that bring comfort and encouragement. A few of mine include: *"Have I not commanded you? Be strong and courageous. Do not be terrified; do not be discouraged, for the LORD your God will be with you wherever you go"* (Joshua 1:9, *NIV*). In Numbers 13 and 14, we recall that God promised the Israelites freedom from Pharaoh's captivity in Egypt, the land of Canaan, which was occupied by powerful people. A reconnaissance mission was sent to spy out the land and report back to the Israelites before occupying the land. The spies returned and indicated that while the land was

indeed marvelous, it was occupied by powerful people. Most of the Israelites were terrified and were afraid of entering the land that God had promised them. However, Joshua and Caleb, who were among the spies of the land, encouraged the Israelites to have faith in God. They stated, "Do not be afraid of the people of the land, because we will swallow them up. Their protection is gone, but the LORD is with us. Do not be afraid of them" (Numbers 14:9, *NIV*). I encourage my patients to consider their freedom from OCD like the land of Canaan and OCD as the powerful people occupying the land. Trust God to help you over-come OCD and help you re-claim your "promised land."

- *Do not be anxious about anything, but in everything, by prayer and petition, with thanksgiving, present your requests to God. And the peace of God, which transcends all understanding, will guard your hearts and your minds in Christ Jesus"* (Philippians 4:6-7, *NIV*).

- *"Where is your faith?' he asked his disciples. In fear and amaze-ment they asked one another, 'Who is this? He commands even the winds and the water, and they obey him'"* (Luke 8:25, *NIV*). I like the metaphor of the disciples in the boat as a sudden storm came upon them in the middle of a lake. This is much like the sudden anxiety that grips peo-ple in the midst of an obsessive thought. The disciples feared they would drown, but when they woke Jesus, he immediately calmed the storm and made it clear that they were safe. I ask patients to remember that the same Lord that calmed the waves and wind can help calm their anxiety and fear.

2. Visualization and Imagery

- The above scriptures can bring confidence, courage, and comfort. They can seem even more powerful when we visualize the concepts. For example, I ask patients to visualize Jesus awaking in a boat, stretching out his hands, and commanding the storm to stop. The truth of scripture coupled with a powerful image can be helpful during moments of anxiety.

- I also ask patients to visualize and imagine clearly what their life would be like free from OCD. Earlier, I discussed establishing treatment goals, one of which included imagining life without OCD. Having a clear image of life free from OCD can also be helpful during the critical interval.

3. Distraction

- I mentioned earlier that distraction can be extremely helpful during the 20 to 30 minutes of the critical interval. I have had patients tell me that they have been successful engaging with pets; surfing the Internet; reading; etc., during this time. Any activity that takes their minds off the obsessive thought or situation can be helpful and can increase the likelihood of success during the critical interval.

4. Having a Supportive Coach Available

- For children, I teach parents about E/RP and tell them that they will have to encourage their children to resist the compulsive behaviors. Few children will attempt this without parental encouragement. During the critical interval, parents must be supportive and remind the child that the anxiety they are feeling will go away soon. They will have to act like a good coach, encouraging their child through a tough time and urging them on to victory. Simple, but confident reassuring statements such as, "I know this is hard for you, but I know you can do it;" or "Remember that each time you resist you are beating OCD" can be very helpful. At times, I encourage parents to play a favorite game with their child to help distract him or her. It is also perfectly acceptable to offer tangible reinforcements or rewards for successfully resisting a compulsion. After all, E/RP is hard work and facing significant fears is not an easy task. Find a tangible way to help a child cooperate with E/RP. One example from my practice involved a young boy who agreed that he would work for a new computer game by complying with E/RP homework. He and his parents set up a system in which he earned 5 points each time he successfully resisted an urge to engage in a specific compulsive behavior. As soon as he earned 100 points, he would earn the game he previously chose to work for. A copy of the advertisement for the game was taped to the refrigerator door. He was given a poker chip which served as a 5-point piece. He enjoyed earning the poker chips, and as he saw his pile of chips increase, he was motivated to continue toward his goal. When he earned enough points for the goal, a new goal and prize was established. The number of points and size of the prize can vary depending upon how difficult the task of resisting may be. Another way parents can help children with resistance is to model the behavior. For example, a parent may expose herself to the same anxiety-producing stimulus that causes the child to become anxious and feel the need to perform a compulsive behavior.

Then, the parent may model that she is not performing the compulsive behavior and asks the child to do the same. This often makes it easier for children to accomplish RP than asking them to do it on their own.

For adults, points and prizes may not be very effective; however, having a supportive coach can be. Many people with OCD do not share their struggles with many people. I encourage my patients to have at least 1 or 2 close friends or family members that they confide in who can serve as supportive coaches, encouragers, and prayer partners. It is important to select these people carefully. While it is not important for them to have complete knowledge of OCD, it is helpful for them to understand something about this disorder. This book is also written in a way that friends and family members can become more educated about OCD. These confidants are good people to call during the critical interval in order to get some encouragement.

5. Journal

- There will inevitably be times when another person may not be available to talk with during the critical interval. In such times, it may be helpful to have a journal in order to write out some thoughts and to do some self-talk. For example, it may be helpful to write down things such as, "As difficult as this is right now, I know that if I hold out for another 20 to 30 minutes, I'll start feeling better and will be glad I didn't give in to the compulsive behavior. Getting free from OCD is worth a few minutes of anxiety, and each time I resist, OCD gets weaker and I get stronger." I also encourage patients to have some of their favorite scripture verses written in the inside cover of their journal, or on an index card in their pocket to refer to quickly.

Slow and Specific

With RP, patients should continue to practice this technique with the lowest level anxiety-producing situation until that situation no longer creates anxiety and causes them to feel the need to perform a compulsive behavior. For some, it may take only a few times of RP to accomplish this. For others, it may take several trials. There is no time limit when using RP. As the patient masters the item on their list with the lowest anxiety value, they then take on the next item. This gradual increase in anxiety producing items will feel natural and is much like starting an exercise program. I usually tell a patient who is discouraged by their list of items to be confronted that if their goal were to run a marathon, they would not start training by going for a 26-mile run. They would start very slowly in order to build up strength and endurance. Once jogging half a mile felt comfortable, they would gradually increase their distance week by week until they felt that running the marathon was easily within their abilities. The same is true of E/RP. The rule of thumb is to always start with a goal that both the patient and therapist feel is realistic. Each stage of progress will make the next goal seem more and more realistic until the items that are higher on the list do not seem as overwhelming.

Different Forms of Resistance

For some patients, beginning E/RP is difficult even for the least anxiety-producing situation. I have worked with patients who felt almost powerless to resist even once. For these individuals, I try to help them find *anything* about the compulsive behavior that they can resist. For example, I may ask them to resist the *frequency* of their compulsive behaviors. I worked with a young man who felt the need to say a compulsive prayer as often as several times per minute. Needless to say, OCD was virtually controlling his life. We agreed to begin RP by having him make sure that he waited at least 2 minutes before he repeated the compulsive prayer. This form of resistance did increase his anxiety during the 2-minute interval. However, he was able to wait at least 2 minutes between each compulsive prayer, and eventually found this to be relatively easy. He was beginning to gain a form of control over his compulsive behaviors by waiting even a brief time between each occurrence. Next, he agreed to wait 4 minutes between each prayer until this became relatively easy. We increased the intervals until he was saying the compulsive prayer only twice daily (morning and evening) with relatively little difficulty. Another form of resistance includes resisting the *length* of the compulsive behavior. For example, I worked with a young man with a hand-washing compulsion. He found it almost impossible to resist washing his hands. I inquired further about his hand washing and found that he washed for approximately 40 seconds each time. He agreed that he would probably be able to reduce the amount of time he washed to 30 seconds with relative certainty. While washing only 30 seconds still resulted in significant anxiety (he did not feel that his hands were clean enough after only 30 seconds), he was able to make it through the critical interval of increased anxiety after washing only 30 seconds to the point that he was able to stop after 30 seconds with no increase in anxiety. After this became easy, we agreed to reduce the hand washing to 20 seconds, and so forth until both he and I felt that his hand washing was not excessive. Finally, there may be times when the compulsive behavior that needs to be resisted is *avoidance*. In other words, an anxiety-producing obsessive thought may be leading a person to avoid something. In this case, RP would involve resisting the act of avoidance and confronting the situation. For instance, a patient may have obsessive thoughts about contamination. The compulsive behavior may be to avoid touching a doorknob. In this case, RP would mean the patient would actually touch the doorknob instead of avoiding it. Of course, this may result in a need for a second RP (e.g., touching the doorknob may cause the patient to want to compulsively wash his hands. This would require the patient to resist washing his hands as a second RP).

Random Acts of Resistance
I tell patients that any and every successful attempt to resist the compulsive behavior is helpful and important. Many patients find that they may be successful on one occasion and unsuccessful on another. Additionally, patients may be working on applying E/RP to a specific compulsive behavior, but find that they may be able to resist other compulsions at various times. I strongly encourage my patients to practice these *random acts of resistance* any time they feel like it. After all, each and every successful attempt to resist is a victory.

Cognitive Therapy
As I stated earlier, cognitive therapy is based on the assumption that the way we think about things determines our response to them. Cognitive therapy is designed to help patients identify thoughts that are illogical, irrational, and/or

unhealthy in order to change or modify them to become more logical, rational, and healthy. Cognitive therapy is not uniquely used to treat OCD. In fact, cognitive therapy is used frequently to help people in a variety of ways. However, cognitive therapy (CT) can be particularly helpful in the treatment of OCD.

Cognitive therapists refer to *errors in thinking* that individuals make routinely. A few examples of errors in thinking include the following:

- *Emotional reasoning*—this refers to reaching conclusions based upon feelings rather than facts. For example, a person with OCD shakes hands with a person he just met and *feels* contaminated, therefore he believes that he *is* contaminated. The *fact* that shaking hands with a person cannot possibly contaminate the person is not considered over the person's *feelings.*

- *Catastrophizing*—this refers to imagining the worst-case scenario of a situation and reacting to the imagined "catastrophe" rather than the actual situation. For example, a person with OCD worries about a family member traveling by airplane. They imagine the worst-case scenario being a plane crash that kills everyone on board. Their anxiety level matches the imagined catastrophe rather than the fact that nothing has happened.

- *Dichotomous thinking*—this refers to the tendency to think in absolute terms (either-or thinking). For example, a person with OCD may have unrealistic perfectionistic standards for performance. Anything short of perfection is experienced and viewed as a failure.

- *Personalization*—this belief refers to the tendency to make everything that happens somehow related to the person (i.e., "everything's my fault"). I worked with a patient who always believed that it was wrong to litter. While this is not an uncommon belief, this particular patient became obsessive about it to the point of developing a checking compulsion to make sure she had not littered. One day she accidentally left a fast-food bag of trash on the top of her car as she drove away. She intended to put the trash in her car in order to throw it in the garbage when she arrived home. However, she forgot it was on top of her car and "accidentally littered." Unfortunately, this happened on a day when an unfortunate accident occurred to one of her friends. She had a difficult time not connecting the two events and not feeling responsible for the accident.

- *Selective Attention*—this type of cognitive error refers to the tendency of a person to notice and consider only certain aspects (usually negative) of a situation. For example, a patient receives the results of his annual physical which indicates that the patient is in very good health. All lab work is normal and the doctor found nothing to be concerned about. However, the doctor tells the patient that he would like for him to work on losing 5 to 10 pounds over the next year for overall maintenance of health. The patient walks away and focuses only on the fact that "My doctor tells me I'm too fat."

These are just a few examples of the more obvious and common errors in thinking that occur. However, almost everyone makes subtle errors in thinking from time to time. People with OCD frequently respond to irrational or distorted beliefs or patterns in thinking. For people with OCD, cognitive distortions often involve such areas as:

- overestimating negative outcome in situations
- exaggerations of "normal" concerns about situations
- owning too great a share of responsibility for the outcome of situations
- having unrealistic expectations for performance

Most irrational or illogical beliefs are automatic and unconscious. In other words, most of the time, a person is not even aware that he or she is reacting to errors in thinking. In fact, it is not uncommon for a person to make more than one cognitive error at a time in the same situation. One of the goals of therapy of OCD is to help the patient realize when he/she is responding to a cognitive error in order to understand how their feelings and behaviors are based upon faulty thinking.

Two popular forms of cognitive therapy, based on the theory that our distorted thoughts and beliefs cause problems in thinking and behaving, include *Rational Emotive Therapy (RET)* developed by Albert Ellis, and a form of cognitive therapy developed by Aaron Beck which focuses on challenging automatic negative thoughts.

RET works on the following model:

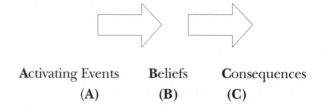

Activating Events   **B**eliefs   **C**onsequences
(A)   **(B)**   **(C)**

In the diagram, Activating Events (A) refers to any situation that causes anxiety; Beliefs (B) refers to one's thoughts about (A); and Consequences (C) refers to the feelings and behaviors one has about (A). In this model, a person is shown that all feelings and behaviors in response to any situation are determined not by the situation, but by the beliefs one has about the situation. RET involves teaching a patient to identify the beliefs (thoughts) he has about situations that cause anxiety. The patient is then taught to discern which thoughts are illogical, irrational, or contain errors in thinking. Finally, the patient is taught to rationally dispute the distorted thoughts by challenging them directly. According to RET, when patients learn to do this effectively, their reactions (C) to events that previously caused anxiety will change as a result.

Aaron Beck's form of cognitive therapy is similar to RET in that it also teaches patients that their thinking influences their reactions to situations. Beck's cognitive therapy also encourages patients to identify their beliefs, but teaches patients that most of the thinking that causes difficulty for them is due to automatic negative thoughts that are broad and inclusive. Examples might include: "I am an unworthy person and people would reject me if they really got to know me" or "I am incompetent and will ultimately fail at anything I attempt." Identifying these automatic negative thoughts is essential to changing a person's reaction to a situation.

Combining E/RP with Cognitive Therapy: The Four R's

Because E/RP and cognitive therapy have been found effective for treatment of OCD, I always use both techniques to treat patients. I have developed a technique known as the

Four R's to help patients remember the essential elements of beating OCD.

1. ***Recognize:*** This step uses cognitive therapy tools to enable the patient to identify the thinking that is behind the anxiety. In treating OCD, this inevitably results in identifying the obsessive thought, worry, or image and correctly defining it as an irrational obsessive thought.

2. ***Resist:*** This step refers to RP in the Response Prevention diagram. In this step, the patient is aware of the urge to perform a compulsive behavior. He has been educated regarding the importance of employing RP as essential in breaking the power of OCD and is prepared to resist the urge to perform the compulsive behavior.

3. ***Replace:*** In step 3, the patient begins the process of modifying the obsessive thought or worry with one that is based on truth.

4. ***Re-direct:*** In the final step, the patient is taught to use the tools mentioned earlier to get through the critical interval of response prevention until the anxiety passes and the pattern of obsessive thoughts followed by compulsive behaviors is weakened.

The Four R's (Recognize; Resist; Replace; Re-direct) sounds easy, but is actually a simplified model that requires the individual to have a great deal of knowledge about the techniques used to treat OCD including understanding the principles behind response prevention as well as the theory of cognitive therapy. Once a patient becomes familiar with these concepts, the Four R's is an easy way to remember how to employ these new tools. Learning this method of treatment requires homework assignments; keeping journal entries of thoughts and behavior patterns; and lots of trial and error. It is a process that takes time, but is ultimately effective in treating OCD.

Just as there are tools for helping patients tolerate the critical interval of E/RP, there are some tools to help patients with the cognitive aspects of treating OCD.

False Alarms

I recall having a conversation with a patient who was struggling with anxiety in my office one afternoon when outside the office building a very loud car alarm sounded. It occurred to me that neither of us gave it much thought as we were both accustomed to many "false car alarms" living in Atlanta. I used the experience to illustrate a point. I asked my patient, "Do you hear that car alarm outside?" She responded, "Sure, but those things go off all the time, and usually they don't mean anything. I don't even know why people bother having them." I explained that her anxiety alarms were similar to that car alarm. In other words, she seemed to have a very sensitive alarm system that triggered even when there was no obvious danger. I tried to explain that one of her goals was going to be to learn how to stop responding each time the alarm sounded—much like she was able to ignore the car alarm outside my office. "It is essential that you re-train your brain to sound the alarm only when there is an actual threat or emergency instead of randomly and for no ostensible reason." This analogy helped her to question and evaluate when her alarm sounded to determine whether there was a real threat or not.

Weeds in the Garden

Atlanta's mild climate usually means at least a few hours of yard work on Saturday about nine months of the year. One day, I was in my yard when I noticed some weeds growing in an area. I recall thinking to myself, "Where in the world do these weeds come from? I didn't plant them." Then I realized that it did not matter where they came from, they simply had to go. I use this analogy to describe obsessive thoughts, worries, and images. Patients usually want to know, "Where are these thoughts coming from?" Often, they fear that there is some deep dark psychological problem or secret that is causing these thoughts. I explain that OCD does not work this way. Remember, OCD is a problem in which the brain sends random thoughts, worries, and images for *no particular reason*. They need to be treated like weeds in the garden. In other words, you did not plant them or ask for them to be there. In fact, it does not really matter why they are there—they simply have to go. This helps patients to avoid the tendency to go on a psychic archeological dig to try and find out what is causing these obsessive thoughts which will ultimately make them worse. I explain that using E/RP is like pulling up a weed and moving on.

Confronting Specific Cognitive Distortions

Scripture tells us in John 8:31-32 (*NIV*) "If you hold to my teaching, you are really my disciples. Then you will know the truth, and the truth will set you free." 2 Corinthians 10:5 (*NIV*) tells us, "...we take captive every thought to make it obedient to Christ." I use these scripture references to help patients understand the importance of cognitive therapy in the treatment of OCD. It is important to recognize the truth of our thinking as opposed to simply accepting our cognitive distortions as fact. Also, we do have the ability to "take our thoughts captive;" (i.e., we can control what we think if we work at it).

For some of the more common cognitive distortions, I give patients some tools to confront these distortions in order to help them with the third step of the Four R's, replacing cognitive distortions with the truth. For example:

1. *Emotional Reasoning:* Your feelings are like a faulty navigation system on an airplane. Most pilots know that you can fly an airplane by determining your direction and location from objects on the ground, or by using instrumentation on the control panel. At night, or in inclement weather, you don't have much choice but to rely on instrumentation. I explain that for many people, feelings are an unreliable source for drawing conclusions. Recall that in emotional reasoning, people reach conclusions based upon how they feel rather than on facts. Therefore, I encourage patients to question their feelings and to make sure that they draw conclusions about situations based on the facts rather than on their emotions which will often lead them astray.

2. *Catastrophizing:* Recall that this refers to reacting to the imagined worst-case scenario. I encourage my patients to make sure that they are living in the *"what is"* instead of in the *"what if."* Many people with OCD find themselves living in the future rather than in the present. In my experience, at least 90 percent of the things people with an

anxiety disorder worry *might* happen never actually happens at all. I think Jesus illustrated this point best when he said, "Therefore do not worry about tomorrow, for tomorrow will worry about itself. Each day has enough trouble of its own" (Matthew 6:34, *NIV*). Another tool that is useful for people who tend to "catastrophize" is called *probability estimation*. In probability estimation, the person is asked to estimate the likelihood that a particular event will actually occur. Through logically evaluating the probability of something happening, the person often reaches the conclusion that they are worrying about something that has a remote chance of actually happening.

3. *Dichotomous thinking:* For people who tend to think in only two categories, I try to help them create a "third file" for thinking about things. I explain that it is as if they have two files for the things in their lives: one for one extreme and one for the other extreme. I further explain that most of the things in their lives actually fit best into a third file that is somewhere between the two extremes. One example of this involves performance expectations. As we discussed earlier, OCD patients often have perfectionistic tendencies. They see their performance in a diagram that looks something like this:

Perfect
Failure

In the diagram, there are only two categories of performance: perfect and failure. Because perfection is difficult, and sometimes impossible to attain, these individuals usually feel that their performance is a failure. I explain that this model is unrealistic and needs to be modified to create a third category:

Perfect
Good enough
Failure

In the revised diagram, a third category called "good enough" has been added to the model. In this model, perfection is still present, as is failure. However, failure is a much smaller category now, and the largest area is "good enough." Most of our performance is, in fact, good enough—not perfect, but certainly acceptable. Creating a third category enables the perfectionist to accept their less than perfect performance without feeling like a failure.

For patients with OCD, third categories need to be established in many different areas in order to avoid the dichotomous thinking errors that exacerbate anxiety and obsessiveness.

4. Personalization: For this type of cognitive error, I encourage patients to challenge the belief that all things that happen are related to or caused by them. For example, I encourage patients to consider whether there is sufficient evidence to indict them for the crime they feel they committed. I use the example of "putting OCD on trial" instead of them. Most of the time, a person with OCD will feel responsible for something when there is no evidence that they are responsible. They need to reconsider the evidence which involves rationally and logically evaluating their conclusion that they are somehow responsible for the negative outcome they feel responsible for.

5. *Selective attention:* For this type of cognitive error, it is important to get and keep a perspective. Recall that in selective attention, the person has a filter that results in ignoring some aspects of a situation and focusing only on the negative aspects of it. I explain that selective attention is like viewing a situation through a camera lens that is focused to only one small aspect of the picture. In this case, the only thing the person is going to see is what the camera lens is focused on. It is important to back up the lens in order to allow the picture to contain all aspects of the scene in order to get an accurate view of the situation.

Of course, these are only a few of the types of cognitive errors that people frequently make. Treating a patient with OCD involves teaching people to *recognize* (Step 1 of the Four R's) the types of thinking that cause problems and teaching them to *replace* (Step 3 of the Four R's) the distorted thinking with the truth.

Habituation

I will never forget my first job in a hospital in Atlanta. The hospital was located across the street from a sewage treatment plant, and the odor was consistent with the nature of the plant. When I first started working there, I recall thinking that the smell was unbearable. However, after a few weeks of working there, each employee *habituated* to the smell. In other words, after being exposed to the smell consistently for long enough, it no longer bothered us. This principle of habituation applies to more than smells. It also works with anxiety. If a person is exposed to an anxiety-provoking stimulus for long enough, then the person will no longer become anxious around the stimulus. This is part of what is happening during RP. The person is not avoiding the feared obsessive thought, but instead is staying with it without performing the compulsive behavior which previously made the obsessive thought disappear for a while. If the patient allows herself to remain with an obsessive thought without "escaping" for long enough, he will habituate to the thought and it will no longer cause anxiety.

Habituation is important for some types of thoughts, images, and mental compulsions (those that involve doing something in your mind as opposed to a specific behavior). It can be very effective to ask a patient to think of an anxiety-producing thought or image consciously and to continue to think about it (without performing any compulsive behaviors) until the anxiety level subsides. This is a type of forced E/RP and can be very effective in reducing the anxiety-producing power of some types of obsessive thoughts.

Non-pharmacological treatment of OCD is highly effective in reducing the symptoms of OCD. In fact, some amazing research has shown that non-pharmacological treatment can actually result in biochemical changes in the brain of OCD patients. PET scans have shown decreased activity in the orbital frontal region of the brain in OCD patients who received behavior therapy. In the final chapter, I will describe two case studies that illustrate how these treatment approaches have been used to treat OCD in specific cases. Non-pharmacological treatment of OCD is not the only treatment shown to be effective in treating OCD. There are times when medication is indicated in the treatment of OCD. In the next chapter, I will discuss how medication is used and when to consider using it as an option.

EIGHT

Treatment of OCD Using Medication

Before writing a chapter on the use of medication to treat OCD, I offer a caveat to the reader. This chapter is for informational purposes only. It is not intended as advice on what medications you should use, or how to use them. Decisions to use medication should be made only after consultation with a physician trained to prescribe and monitor these medications. The information offered in this chapter is to help educate the reader on the role medication can play in the treatment of OCD and to offer specific advice to discuss with your health care professional.

Because OCD is a biological disorder that results from a deficiency in the neurotransmitter serotonin, medications that affect serotonin levels in the brain are highly effective in the treatment of OCD. The types of medications used in the treatment of OCD are generally the medications known as *Selective Serotonin Reuptake Inhibitors (SSRI's)*. These medications work by affecting how the nerve cells of the brain share information with one another. In chapter 3, I briefly discussed how one neuron (nerve cell in the brain) communicates with another. In order to understand how SSRI's work to treat OCD, a more thorough explanation may be necessary.

The brain is made up of billions of nerve cells called *neurons*. These neurons intersect with one another at a tiny space called a *synapse*. The brain sends and receives messages by sending chemicals called *neurotransmitters* from one neuron to another through the synapse. There are many different types of neurotransmitters in the brain; however, the one implicated in OCD is called serotonin.

The diagram below may help to illustrate how this process works:

A Synapse

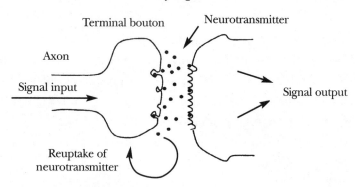

In the diagram above, the neuron on the left (Sender) is sending a message to the neuron on the right (Receiver). The Sender releases the neurotransmitter into the synapse so that the Receiver will accept the neurotransmitter on its receptor sites. As soon as enough of the neurotransmitter has connected to the receptor sites on the Receiver, the neuron is activated (or "turned on") and the signal is sent. Because the Sender releases more neurotransmitter into the synapse than is needed to activate the Receiver, there is excess neurotransmitter in the synapse that did not find the receptor sites on the Receiver. The Sender releases a transporter protein into the synapse that collects the excess neurotransmitter and takes it back into the Sender for later use. One can think of this as something like a recycling system (i.e., the neurotransmitter that does not get used is saved for later).

The SSRI medications work by blocking the process known as reuptake. In other words, these medications stop the brain's natural recycling process in order to make the neurotransmitter more available in the synapse for the neuron intended to receive the serotonin. The result of this process is that the serotonin receptor sites on the Receiver neuron are stimulated in order to make them more active. This results in an increase in activity on the receptor sites of the Receiver neuron.

Research and clinical experience show that treatment with the SSRI medications is very effective in reducing symptoms of OCD. However, it should be noted that these medications do not *cure* OCD, but instead reduce the symptoms of the disorder. Many patients ask which form of treatment is more effective in treating OCD: medication or the non-pharmacological treatments. The answer is both. Research shows that non-pharmacological treatment alone is roughly equivalent in effectiveness to medication alone. However, the best outcome seems to be using the two treatments together.

I find patients have a variety of feelings and attitudes regarding medication. Upon learning that medication can be a helpful treatment modality, some patients become extremely excited and want to immediately pursue that option. On the other hand, some patients have a strong bias against the use of medications and are extremely reticent to consider this approach. Frequently, a patient will elect to try non-pharmacological techniques before considering medication. There are a variety of reasons including concern about side effects of medication; cost of medication; or simply a reticence to take medication in general. It is appropriate to attempt non-pharmacological treatments if you are still able to function adequately in the primary roles of your life; there are no significant co-morbid conditions; and you are willing to tolerate some increased anxiety from the E/RP mentioned in the last chapter.

The decision to use medication to treat OCD is ultimately one made by a treating physician after carefully assessing the patient's condition and considering the best course of treatment. I usually recommend considering medication to treat OCD symptoms in the following situations:

When OCD is so severe that it is causing significant impairment in the person's functioning. For example, a student is unable to perform in school; an adult is unable to perform adequately in his or her job; or an individual is suffering severe social impairment due to the intensity and severity of OCD symptoms.

When a person has attempted non-pharmacological treatment but is unable to tolerate the increase in anxiety that is inherent in this form of therapy.

When a patient has severe co-morbid depression or panic attacks and is unable to participate in or benefit from non-pharmacological treatment without the use of medication.

When a child's symptoms are having a significant effect on the family functioning (e.g., frequent battles over getting ready in the morning or completing homework).

When a patient asks for medication to relieve symptoms. As a professional, it is unethical to deny a viable treatment option from a patient if he or she asks for it. My colleague and friend, Dr. John Lochridge, coined the term "misery line" to describe the intangible point at which a patient becomes so "miserable" that he needs a more acute and immediate treatment alternative such as medication. When a patient or family has crossed the "misery line" and asks for medication, it is appropriate to refer them to a physician trained to diagnose and treat OCD with medication.

Should you and your physician decide that medication is an appropriate treatment for your OCD, there are a few things to consider. First, not everyone responds to the same medication in the same way. Each of us carries a miraculous genetic map that only our Creator fully understands. Science can give us only a partial understanding of how the brain works. While the illustration I used earlier to describe how neurons in the brain communicate with one another using neurotransmitters sounds simple, the reality is that the brain's interconnecting pathways and neurotransmitter systems are incredibly elegant and complex. There are so many individual differences among people that it is not unusual for two different people with almost identical symptoms to experience very different results from the same drug. Fortunately, there are several different SSRI medications. Consequently, if you do not experience efficacy from one, you may find a different one to be effective.

Second, while medications used to treat OCD are usually effective, they do not work immediately. Typically, it takes from four to ten weeks before full benefit can be experienced. Furthermore, some patients actually report that their symptoms worsen initially after starting medication before they begin to improve. This phenomenon is due to an initial over-stimulation of the post-synaptic serotonin receptors on the Receiver neuron. It may be difficult to wait the full 4 to 10 weeks for improvement, particularly if you experience a worsening of symptoms initially.

Third, all medications have side effects, and SSRI's are no exception. Later, I will describe the primary medications used to treat OCD and list specific side effects of each. However, almost all SSRI's can result in the following side effects:

- sexual problems including decreased desire; delayed orgasm; and difficulty with achieving orgasm
- nausea (usually disappears after a few weeks)
- weight gain
- fatigue
- daytime sedation

The most common and annoying side effects of the SSRI medications seem to be the sexual side effects (decreased libido); apathy/decreased motivation; and weight gain. Many patients report emotional blunting on higher doses of SSRI medications.

Fourth, even if medication works well to reduce OCD symptoms, without coupling this with non-pharmacological treatment as described in Chapter seven, the symptoms of OCD tend to return when the medication is discontinued. It is best to think of medication as an *adjunct* to treatment rather than a complete treatment choice.

Finally, the decision to use medication must always be made with consideration to the other health issues of the individual. SSRI medications are usually safe to take with other medications. However, all drug interactions should be discussed fully with your physician. For individuals who consume alcohol, the SSRI medications can significantly reduce tolerance to alcohol, and alcohol consumption can decrease the effectiveness of these medications. All drug interactions should be discussed with your doctor.

The United States Food and Drug Administration has approved five medications for the treatment of OCD. I will list each and describe typical dosing information and possible side effects. It should be noted that not everyone experiences the side effects listed with each medication. In addition, some people tend to compare the doses used and erroneously think that the one that uses the lowest dose will be better, safer, etc. Comparing milligrams is not helpful as each of these medications works in a slightly different way. For example, taking 200 mg of Zoloft is not taking "more" medication than taking 40 mg of Prozac. It is comparing apples to oranges to compare doses in this fashion. Here are the five medications that have received FDA approval in the treatment of OCD.

Anafranil (clomipramine)

Anafranil is a medication specifically designed to treat OCD. It is actually not an SSRI, but an SNRI (*Serotonin-Norepinephrine Reuptake Inhibitor*). This means that the medication affects the neurotransmitter norepinephrine as well as serotonin; however, the predominant effect of clomipramine is on serotonin. The typical dosage range is 150-250 mg daily. Side effects can include dry mouth; sedation; fatigue; tremor; dizziness; increased heart rate; constipation; sexual dysfunction; and weight gain.

Prozac (fluoxetine)

While Prozac is better known for its effectiveness in treating depression, it is also efficacious in the treatment of OCD. The typical dosage range is higher in treating OCD than for treating depression alone. The usual dose for the treatment of depression may be 10-20 mg daily. However, in treating OCD, the dosage may be from 20-80 mg daily. Side effects can include nervousness; agitation; apathy; nausea; diarrhea; weight gain; headache; dry mouth; tremors; and sexual dysfunction.

Zoloft (sertraline)

Zoloft is also known in the treatment of depression. The typical dosage for the treatment of OCD is 50 to 200 mg daily. Side effects can include diarrhea; tremor; dry mouth; insomnia; nausea; anorexia; ejaculation failure in men; increased sweating; sexual dysfunction; and weight gain.

Paxil (paroxetine)

Paxil is marketed for the treatment of social anxiety disorder; panic disorder; and depression. It is also used to treat OCD. The typical dosage for the treatment of OCD is 40 to 80 mg daily. Side effects can include frequent urination; weakness; fatigue; dizziness; sweating; nausea; somnolence; headache; sexual dysfunction; and constipation.

Luvox (fluvoxamine)

The typical dosage for treatment of OCD is 200-300 mg daily. Side effects can include drowsiness; constipation; anorexia; insomnia; nausea; somnolence; abnormal ejaculation in men; nervousness; sexual dysfunction; and dry mouth.

When selecting a particular medication to treat OCD, your physician will choose the particular medication based upon your particular symptoms and individual history. Do not be discouraged if the first medication is not effective. Failure of one medication to reduce symptoms does not predict lack of efficacy in a different one. I have seen many patients experience no obvious benefit from one medication but find significant benefit when their treatment protocol included a change to a different one. There is really no way to predict which medication will work for which patient. One exception may be when a first-degree relative has been successfully treated with a particular medication. In this case, it is common for the physician to prescribe the same medication that was effective for a family member. This may be because genetic similarity predicts similar response to a medication.

While the five medications discussed above are the ones typically used in the treatment of OCD, they are by no means the only ones used. A physician may choose to treat OCD with other antidepressant medications. Examples of ones used include *Celexa (citalopram); Effexor XR (venlafaxine); Remeron (mirtazapione); and Lexapro (escitalopram)*. Your doctor may also discuss adding a medication in order to augment treatment (increase the effectiveness of the medication) with Anafranil or one of the SSRI medications. Such medications used for this purpose include *Buspar (buspirone)*. Occasionally, a type of medication known as *anxiolytics* (anti-anxiety medications) may be used with other medications if you are experiencing debilitating panic attacks. Examples of these types of medications include *Xanax (alprazolam); Ativan (lorazepam); or Klonopin (clonazepam)*. Less commonly used, but occasionally seen in the treatment of OCD, are the use of antipsychotic medications such as *Risperdal (risperidone)* and *Zyprexa (olanzapine)* or mood-stabilizing medications such as *Depakote (valproic acid); Neurontin (gabapentin); or lithium (brand names include Eskalith or Lithobid)*. When patients with OCD have co-morbid Tourette's disorder, *Orap* may be used. Because ADHD is a frequent co-morbid disorder with OCD, it is not uncommon for patients to be treated with both an SSRI and a stimulant medication if both diagnoses are present. Finally, for some side effects such as sexual dysfunction, your doctor may discuss additional medications to minimize or treat the side effects.

I would like to close this chapter with some frequently asked questions concerning the use of medication in the treatment of OCD:

1. *"If I choose to take medication, how long will I have to take it?"*

    As I stated earlier, you should think of medication to treat OCD as an adjunct to be used along with non-pharmacological treatments discussed in Chapter seven. There is no definitive answer for how long you may need to use medication. This is a decision you make with your physician. Several variables factor into this decision including your response to non-pharmacological treatment; your tolerance of the medication; other health issues; severity of symptoms; and your compliance with and comfort with taking the medication. Typically, you should prepare to take the medications for a period of 12-18 months. You should never stop taking medication abruptly or without the advice of your doctor as this could result in SSRI discontinuation syndrome which is characterized by nausea, dizziness, and severe headache. This usually lasts from 3 to 7 days before the symptoms disappear.

2. *"I am seeing a therapist for non-pharmacological treatment of my OCD. If I want to take medication, I will need to see a physician. Does this mean I will have to change therapists?"*

No. It is common to have a therapist to work on the non-pharmacological treatment of OCD and to have a physician to prescribe and monitor medication. Medication management does not usually require frequent appointments once a maintenance dose is reached. Some physicians are trained to use both medication and non-pharmacological treatments. Therefore, it is possible to use the same physician for both forms of treatment. However, it is more common to have a separate therapist for non-pharmacological treatment and a physician to manage medication therapy.

3. *"Can any doctor prescribe medication for OCD?"*

Any physician licensed by the state in which you live can prescribe medications for OCD. You should discuss the physician's experience, knowledge, and comfort with treating OCD before deciding to use him or her for this purpose. Typically a psychiatrist will have the most experience with treating OCD. However, physicians in other specialties may have a great deal of interest and experience as well. If you have trouble finding a professional, you may want to check with the OC Foundation (www.ocfoundation.org). Do not hesitate to ask your doctor specific questions.

4. *"My doctor is recommending a specific medication to treat my OCD, but my insurance company does not cover this drug. What should I do?"*

You should discuss this with your doctor. Give your doctor information about your particular insurance coverage so he or she will know which medications are covered and which are not.

5. *"I've heard that Prozac makes people suicidal. Is this true?"*

There are many "myths and legends" concerning the types of medications used to treat OCD, depression, and other psychiatric disorders. Most of these "disaster stories" are based more on rumor and hysteria than fact. The answer is no. Neither Prozac nor any of the medications listed above have been shown to cause people to become suicidal, homicidal, or in any way dangerous when taken appropriately under the supervision of a physician. It should be noted that these types of medications should *not* be mixed with alcohol or other drugs as results can be unpredictable.

6. *"My child has severe OCD and they are recommending medication to treat her. I'm concerned that this will interfere with her development. Should I worry?"*

I would worry more that not treating the OCD could interfere with her normal development. OCD in childhood can interfere with academic functioning; social functioning; and increases the chances of depression and self-esteem problems. Empirical studies have not demonstrated negative effects from these medications on normal childhood development. You may want to try non-pharmacological treatments if you have not done so before considering medication. However, if a professional is recommending medication, I would encourage you to strongly consider it as an option.

7. *"I'm concerned that these medications will change my personality."*

I know people who wish that these medications *did* result in personality changes. However, they do not. The only thing these medications do is affect the level of neurotransmitters in the brain. Because they can be dramatically effective in symptom reduction, you may observe a noticeable change in your mood and behavior. However, it is more likely that OCD caused a change from your normal personality and the benefits of medication will help you return to a more normal presentation.

8. *"I have a friend who has been taking one of these medications for years. Should I be concerned about him?"*

Not unless he is not being monitored by a physician. I stated earlier that one should be prepared to take SSRI to treat OCD for around 12 to 18 months. Many patients can discontinue the medication (under the supervision of their doctor) without a remission of symptoms. However, there are some patients who need to take these medications for much longer. This decision is one made in consultation with your physician. There are no definitive long-term studies that unequivocally demonstrate the safety of long-term use of these medications. Part of the reason for this is that such controlled studies are very difficult to conduct. However, there is presently no data to suggest that long term use of these medications is nefarious.

9. *"I'm not very good at remembering to take medication. How is it administered and how often do you have to take it?"*

All of these medications are administered orally. Some of them come in a liquid form if swallowing a tablet or capsule is difficult (as it is for some OCD patients). The dosing is different from one medication to another. Most are taken once daily, and Prozac comes in a form that is taken once weekly.

10. *"As a Christian, I just don't feel right about taking a medication like this."*

Why not? God chooses to heal through different methods. He has blessed us with many different medications to treat a variety of illnesses from ear infections to cancer to depression to OCD. I believe that God has allowed us to gain an understanding of how the brain works so that we can help those suffering from illnesses like OCD. I would encourage you to think of medication as one of God's many gifts to his children to alleviate your suffering.

It is my hope that this chapter will provide the reader with specific information so that the option of medication can be considered with more accurate data. In the next and final chapter, I will describe some actual clinical cases from my practice that illustrate how OCD manifests in an individual and how the treatment options I have described in the last two chapters have worked for these individuals.

NINE

Case Studies

In this chapter, I will describe two actual cases of people who have seen me for the treatment of OCD. I have changed some identifying information in order to protect the confidentiality of each individual. However, each case is authentic and illustrates how OCD can manifest as well as how it can be treated.

Mandy

Mandy was a college student who came to see me because her personal physician recognized that she was showing symptoms of OCD. When I asked her to tell me about her symptoms, she told me that she "constantly worried." She also described some significant compulsive behaviors. For example:

- She stated that she had to open and close her locker 44 times which caused her to be late for class.
- She described having to have things pointed in certain directions.
- She had to carry pictures of her family members with her at all times. If she left her house without these pictures, she would have to return and get them.
- She frequently said a specific prayer of protection over her family members. This was the same prayer said exactly the same way. Saying the prayer brought

temporary relief from anxiety that harm might befall her family members; however, the prayer had to be repeated so frequently it became cumbersome.

- She had to honk the horn a certain number of times when she left her house or when she drove past her house. She feared that if she did not, something would happen to one of her family members.

- If she was with a friend that she cared for or with a family member, she had to say "see you" rather than good-bye; and the other person had to say "see you" in return.

- She often became fixated on a certain number. Then she would have to do things that number of times. For example, if the number was 5, she would have to pump the soap dispenser 5 times; she would have to dry her hand with 5 paper towels; etc.

Mandy's symptoms were interfering with her daily life to a significant degree. Therefore, I suggested that medication might be an appropriate treatment option initially in order to reduce her symptoms more immediately. She was receptive to the option of medication. Therefore, I referred Mandy to a physician for a medication evaluation. He prescribed a medication to treat her symptoms of OCD. Unfortunately, she was unable to swallow the pills. Consequently, her physician changed her medication to one that could be taken in liquid form, making compliance easier.

I asked her to create a list of her compulsive behaviors and to rank them from least to most difficult to resist. I explained how response prevention worked and predicted an increase in her anxiety as she practiced response prevention. After some discussion, Mandy stated that she felt she could start response prevention by limiting her "protection prayer ritual" to once a hour. This would require her to resist saying it as often as she was currently saying this prayer—several times in a hour. We discussed ways to tolerate that anxiety that she felt during the critical interval including distraction (spending time with friends; engaging in some of her favorite activities; or working on a mundane task) and cognitive techniques such as using the four R's: *Recognize; Resist; Replace; and Re-direct.* She was able to *recognize* that the prayer was a compulsive behavior. She was aware of the need to *resist* saying the prayer by limiting it to once every hour. I asked her to *replace* the irrational and erroneous belief that this ritual protection prayer would actually prevent something bad from happening to her friends or family. I asked her to remember that God did not work like a genie in a bottle (e.g., you must state your wish exactly right for it to come true). I asked her to replace this erroneous belief with the truth that God loved her friends and family as much as her and that He would not cause them to be harmed as a result of her not saying a compulsive prayer every few minutes. Finally, Mandy was able to *re-direct* her attention during the critical interval.

Mandy was able to reduce the compulsive prayer to once every hour. In fact, she found that after the first few times of resisting, she was able to do it quite easily. This is true for many OCD patients: once they find an area that they can successfully control, momentum is on their side and they are able to successfully control more of their symptoms. Mandy agreed that she wanted to limit this compulsive behavior even further. She agreed that she would try to limit her prayer to once in the morning and once in the evening. We even discussed that praying for the protection of her friends and family with this frequency was not at all unusual and would probably not qualify as compulsive.

Mandy returned to report that she was not entirely successful at limiting her compulsive prayer to twice daily; however, she was able to consistently limit it to three times daily. Both of us felt that this was an enormous success, particularly given that before she began treatment, she was saying the same compulsive prayer up to a hundred times in one day. Mandy was encouraged and eager to continue to take back control of her life.

The next area she felt that she wanted to work on included her compulsive need to say, "See you" to her friends and family and to have them say "See you" back before she could part from them. Her OCD told her that if this did not happen, something terrible might happen to one of them, and that it would be her fault. This compulsion was more difficult to resist. In fact, Mandy stated that she did not feel that there was any way she could leave without doing this. We decided that we would begin to change this compulsion gradually. Mandy had a cell phone, and I instructed her to have her friends and family (all of whom were aware of Mandy's OCD and who cooperated with her in the "see you" ritual) *not* say "See you" before she left. I asked Mandy to simply say, "See you" and then leave. She was to wait 5 minutes after which she could call the person back who would then say, "See you" over the phone. This was difficult for her, and the anxiety she experienced during the critical interval was significant. However, she recalled the success she had with using response prevention with the compulsive prayer, and she was encouraged enough to work through this anxiety. Once the 5 minute wait became easy, I asked her to lengthen this interval by another 5 minutes, and so on. Eventually, the anxiety dissipated and there was no need to call back at all.

One of the most encouraging things for me, as her clinician, was the session in which she reported that she successfully used RP for a compulsive behavior on her own (i.e., we had not discussed a plan for this particular symptom). Mandy reported that she left her apartment one day and realized, halfway to her destination, that she had forgotten the pictures of her family that she normally carried with her. In the past, this would have resulted in severe anxiety resulting from the obsessive thought that, "If I don't have their picture, something terrible could happen to them and it would be my fault." Mandy used the four R's to deal with this situation. She *recognized* this as an obsessive thought and that going back to get the photos was a compulsive behavior. She *resisted* the urge to go back and get the photographs. She *replaced* the irrational obsessive thought with the truth: "Carrying photographs of my family does not protect them. God is in charge of my family, not me. I will trust Him rather than my own superstitious behavior to protect my family." Finally, she *re-directed* her thoughts and attention to the things she was doing at that moment. It was at this session that I felt Mandy had learned the tools that would help her successfully manage her OCD for her life.

I still see Mandy occasionally. She is aware that OCD is a condition that she will always be predisposed to. We use the analogy of OCD as an uninvited house guest. You don't like the fact that he lives in your house, but he stays there nonetheless. Your goal is to give him one room and one room only. As long as he stays in that room, he is not really that troublesome. If he tries to come into your other rooms, you immediately tell him where he belongs, and you take back the remainder of your house. Mandy has the tools to keep OCD in his room. Currently, Mandy talks with me about other issues in her life, many of which have nothing to do with OCD. She knows that if OCD begins to bother her again, she has tools to deal with it.

Eric

I mentioned Eric in Chapter one on obsessions. Eric was a fifteen-year-old boy who struggled with guilt and shame over any sexual thoughts or feelings. When Eric was about ten years old, he experienced an episode of sexual curiosity and experimentation with another boy. Following this incident, he began to manifest significant symptoms of OCD. Because the symptoms appeared immediately and were not present before the incident, it would be tempting to view the incident as causing the OCD. However, I believe that the incident *triggered* an underlying OCD diathesis that already existed. I find inexperienced therapists often focusing too much on something that they feel caused the OCD instead of recognizing that the OCD would probably have manifested at some point whether the incident occurred or not. The focus should be on the OCD, rather than the precipitating event. In Eric's case, it was important to make sure that the parents of both boys were aware of the incident, and that it was dealt with properly. By the time Eric came to see me, this had already occurred.

When Eric saw me with his parents initially, he had been correctly diagnosed with OCD. His symptoms included the belief that anything associated with sexual thoughts or feelings was "contaminated." He feared that he may have a sexually transmitted disease. This appeared to be an obsessive thought associated with his guilt over the sexual incident from years earlier. He was unable to come in contact with his genitals, even when showering, without going through an elaborate hand-washing ritual. His showers were ritualistic and compulsive as well, taking up to 45 minutes. If he had a nocturnal emission at night, he felt contaminated and had to go through an elaborate cleaning ritual the next morning. His fear of contamination (due to bed sheets) generalized to all dirty laundry, and he was unable to touch or come in contact with laundry. One evening, he was in his basement when he saw a television show that was sexually arousing to him. This triggered significant obsessive thoughts of guilt, and he began to feel that the basement was contaminated. Soon, everything in the basement and everything that came in contact with the basement became contaminated. This was a problem since his bedroom was in the basement. The anxiety was so severe, Eric moved into a guest room on the upper floor of his house. Eric's life was full of anxiety and feelings of contamination.

Eric was miserable, and his very loving and supportive parents were at the end of their rope as well. It was obvious that medication was indicated, and Eric was treated with medication to reduce his symptoms. I explained the process of non-pharmacological treatment to Eric and his parents, and they agreed to try RP to treat his OCD. We decided that it was important for Eric to feel comfortable in his own home. Therefore, I asked Eric to list the areas of his house that he felt were contaminated from least to most. His list clearly indicated that the television in the basement was the source of the "contamination." The television and all areas around it elicited the most anxiety. In fact, one of Eric's favorite hats was placed on a table in the basement beside the television in the basement, causing it to be contaminated. Eric was no longer able to wear this hat.

We started by having Eric expose himself to things that were in the basement. For example, his parents brought up a pillow from the basement. I asked his parents to work with Eric and ask Eric to hold the pillow in his hands for a few minutes which used the four R's. He was able to *recognize* that his fears of contamination were obsessions and that his avoidance of the basement was compulsive. He realized that by holding the pillow he was *resisting* the compulsive behavior, which in this case was avoiding anything associated with the basement. I asked him to *replace* the obsessive and illogical conclusion about contamination with truth (i.e., "Inanimate objects such as pillows are not good or bad. They cannot contaminate me."). Finally, I asked Eric to *re-direct* his attention and thoughts following the exposure and to further *resist* the urge to compulsively wash his hands after holding the object. He found that playing with his dog was a helpful distraction.

Eric was able to "take back" his basement one step at a time. As RP progressed, Eric was asked to perform such exercises as placing his hand on the television for 10 minutes; sitting in the chair in front of the television and watching a television show; etc. Eric successfully "re-claimed" his basement within a few months. There were some rough spots along the way, and Eric, like many OCD patients, found a few steps of the RP hierarchy particularly difficult. Eric was fortunate because his father was a good coach who was able to push and encourage him through the difficult steps.

Even after re-claiming the basement, Eric still had difficulty with accepting normal and healthy sexual thoughts and feelings. In order to help Eric with this area of his life, we applied the four R's again:

1. Eric was to *recognize* that his guilt and fears of contamination associated with normal and healthy sexual thoughts and feelings were symptoms of his OCD.
2. Eric was to *resist* his compulsive behaviors that usually followed his obsessive thoughts. These compulsive behaviors included: compulsively washing his hands; compulsive rituals in his shower; and avoiding contact with clothing and bed sheets following nocturnal emissions.
3. Eric was to *replace* his obsessive thoughts with the truth: it is perfectly normal for adolescents to experience sexual thoughts and feelings; nocturnal emissions are a normal part of healthy adolescent development; etc.
4. Finally, Eric was to *re-direct* his attention and behavior as his anxiety increased while he resisted his compulsive behaviors.

Eric was able to begin to accept his sexuality as a normal part of his being—one that was created by God to be accepted; enjoyed; and used to honor God.

These are two brief examples of how OCD can manifest in individuals and how medication and non-pharmacological therapy can be used to help individuals overcome OCD. Perhaps there is no better way to end this book than with an actual letter from a person who overcame OCD. I have re-printed this letter with the individual's permission. It is reprinted verbatim, exactly as it was originally written. I have omitted only the person's name in order to protect her anonymity.

I am twenty-one years old, and I've been dealing with severe, treatment-resistant obsessive-compulsive disorder for over three years now. I believe it is important to share my story so that others will be moved to learn about the disorder, to inspire those suffering with OCD, and show them that help is available.

In my early teen years, I began noticing some symptoms of obsessive-compulsive disorder, though at the time I knew nothing about it. I thought things must be done in a certain way or someone in my family, including myself, would die. These thoughts caused minor distress and soon went away. My next, and most significant, bout with OCD began during the end of my junior year in high school. The obsession, or horrible thoughts, about what could happen in response to my every action grew stronger and stronger. In turn, I began doing more and more compulsions to prevent these terrible things from happening. A compulsion is a ritual or pattern that is done to prevent your most feared thoughts and obsessions from coming true. My fears, or obsessions, can pretty much be placed into the following categories:

1. *someone in my family, including myself and our dog, and my boyfriend, might die*
2. *my boyfriend might break up with me, and finally, the most distressing of all:*
3. *becoming like a "strange" person, for example, homeless people, obese people, people with horrible tempers, and most specifically, gay people.*

I was truly afraid that if I didn't set something in exactly the right place, say, think, or do something a certain number of times, or touch something, even act like a "strange" person, I would cause these horrible things to happen or it would make me like those other people. For others to get an idea of what OCD feels like, they can imagine feeling the need to make sure the stove is turned off; if they do, they could prevent their home from burning down, even save the lives of their pets; if they don't, the feeling of the need to check it will be the only thing on their mind for a long and worrisome period of time. If you take this situation and multiply it by about a hundred, you can only begin to imagine the torture a person suffering from OCD goes through every second of every day.

Obsessive-compulsive disorder can be an extremely hindering, sometimes even paralyzing disorder. To convey this idea, imagine feeling the need to stand in the bathroom washing your hands for ten minutes or more. How about attempting getting dressed for the day, but finally giving up after putting clothes on and immediately taking them off and repeating this for several minutes? These are only some of the many patterns I did to try to control my life. I was also unable to function satisfactorily at school and work. It eventually got so bad that I would stay in bed most of the day just to avoid everyday activities. I began feeling jealous of other people, thinking that, unknowingly, they were taking the tiniest things for granted. Others could just walk in and out of a room once, whereas I might repeat this for minutes at a time. Everyone else could drink just enough of a beverage to quench their thirst, but I would continue doing my patterns, drinking until I would almost feel like gagging. I wanted more than anything in the world to be like everyone else and lead a normal life.

Getting to my goal of leading a normal life, however, is harder than some might think. When my parents accidentally discovered something was wrong, they immediately called our family doctor. He referred us to a psychologist whom he highly recommended. Though she was nice and tried her best, being a general psychologist meant that she lacked the knowledge of how to specifically treat OCD. She referred me to a wonderful psychiatrist. I soon began seeing him. He never let my hopes down of getting better. He tried every combination of medicine thinkable to treat the disorder. At one point, he even put me on morphine. Still, no medicine had a lasting effect.

Having OCD is not an individual battle. Parents or spouses get almost as involved in fighting the disorder as the patient. My parents were definitely, and still are, involved. They went to every doctor's appointment I had and helped me the best they knew how. Unfortunately, OCD is so frustrating that patients and their families can easily lose their tempers with one another. This was definitely true with my family. I can remember many nights, especially early in my treatment, of yelling and crying. We would be so frustrated, not understanding the disorder and being at a complete loss about what to do next. It got so bad that not only was I taking around ten to fifteen pills a day, my mother had to be put on anti-depressants. I felt like all the fighting and my parents' anger and depression was my fault, but I didn't know what to do. Finally at our wits' end, my mother contacted an expert in the research and treatment of OCD. He got in touch with my psychiatrist and recommended that I try behavioral therapy.

Finding a psychologist who specifically uses behavior therapy can be very difficult. Unfortunately, few psychologists specialize in this area. In my case, even though I live near a large city, there were only three behavior therapists even remotely near my home. This is very sad, considering how many millions of people suffer from OCD. I hope I can convey the positive impact these therapists have through my own story. I began going to see my new psychologist in October of 2001. She specifically deals in the research and treatment of anxiety disorders including OCD. She immediately had a positive attitude, but told me the honest details of exposure and response prevention therapy up front.

Though I was terrified about facing my fears head-on and unsure whether I had what it took to battle the OCD using behavior therapy, I decided to try it. My psychologist ended up being just like a friend. For the first time, I was actually able to tell someone all of the "nitty-gritty" details, as she likes to say, about my OCD. From there she guided me through the behavior therapy, encouraging me to expose myself to my fears, but learn how to prevent myself from doing the patterns. She was there every step of the way, encouraging me, and making herself available as often as possible.

The behavior therapy helped me to improve quickly. The rapid improvement of my OCD was a pleasant surprise to my family and me. In about two months we saw major improvement. I would now recommend behavior therapy to anyone suffering from OCD. It may seem unthinkable, even impossible at first, but like my doctor says, you don't believe it until you've actually experienced it.

I am now taking a maintenance dose of OCD medication and going to see my psychologist for regular therapy sessions. In therapy, we check-in on my OCD and talk about things going on in my life in general; things that could create stress and cause an increase in my OCD symptoms. My visits to her have decreased, as have my appointments with my psychiatrist. I never thought I'd see the day when that would happen!

My main hope in writing this is to expose people and educate them about OCD as best I can. The need for more research is great, as is that of psychologists who deal specifically with obsessive-compulsive disorder and behavior therapy. Also, I feel there is a need to educate the general public about OCD. I believe this can be done through television and other forms of media. OCD sufferers need to know that they have a treatable disorder and that they are **not** crazy. (At one time, before I understood what OCD was, I believed I was going crazy.) People *trying to understand and deal with OCD need to know that treatment is definitely available. Through my faith in God and the support from my family and my physicians, I overcame OCD. With a strong faith in God and the right treatment, whether it is by taking medication, going through behavior therapy, or a combination of both, anyone can succeed in fighting obsessive-compulsive disorder.*

Name withheld

I am grateful to this woman for allowing me to publish her letter. I believe that her story is full of hope and encouragement to anyone suffering from OCD.

Even more encouraging is the fact that her story is not unique. I have had the privilege of working with numerous individuals who have similar stories of finding relief from their suffering from OCD symptoms after receiving the appropriate treatment. Few things have been as professionally rewarding for me as celebrating with patients who have experienced relief from OCD symptoms, and seeing their joy return as they reclaim their lives from the prison of OCD.

My sincere prayer is that anyone suffering from OCD who reads this book will courageously seek appropriate help for this treatable biological condition and will experience the same exodus from the bondage of OCD that others have experienced.

References

FOUR

(1) Chansky, Tamar E. *Freeing Your Child from Obsessive-Compulsive Disorder.* New York: Three Rivers Press, 2000.

(2) MMWR, June 9, 2000/ Vol 49/ No. SS-5 U.S. Department of Health and Human Services; CDC; Atlanta, Georgia.

SIX

(1) Penzel, Fred. *Obsessive-Compulsive Disorders: A Complete Guide to Getting Well and Staying Well.* New York: Oxford University Press, 2000.

(2) Dornbush, Marilyn P. & Pruitt, Sheryl K. *Teaching the Tiger: A Handbook for Individuals Involved in the Education of Students with Attention Deficit Disorders, Tourette Syndrome or Obsessive-Compulsive Disorder.* Duarte, CA: Hope Press, 1995.

Resources

The following is a list of resources for individuals affected by obsessive-compulsive disorder and related disorders.

Organizations for OCD

Obsessive-Compulsive Foundation (OCF)
337 Notch Hill Road
North Branford, CT 06971
(203) 315-2190
www.ocfoundation.org

Obsessive-Compulsive Information Center (OCIF)
Madison Institute of Medicine
7617 Mineral Point Road; Suite 300
Madison, WI 53717
(608) 827-2470
www.miminc.org

OC & Spectrum Disorders Association (OCSDA)
18653 Ventura Boulevard; Suite 414
Tarzana, CA 91356
(818) 990-4830
www.ocdhelp.org

Anxiety Disorders Association of America (ADAA)
11900 Parklawn Drive; Suite 100
Rockville, MD 20852-2624
(301) 231-9350
www.adaa.org

Obsessive-Compulsive Anonymous World Services (OCA)
P.O. Box 215
New Hyde Park, NY 11040
(516) 741-4901
members.aol.com/west24th/index.html

Tourette Syndrome Association, Inc. (TSA)
42-40 Bell Boulevard
New York, NY 11361-2874
(718) 224-2999
www.tsa-usa.org

The Trichotillomania Learning Center, Inc. (TLC)
1215 Mission Street; Suite 2
Santa Cruz, CA 95060
(831) 457-1004
www.trich.org

Scrupulous Anonymous (SA)
One Liguori Drive
Liguori, MO 63057-9999
www.liguori.org/newsletters/scrupanon.htm

Books on OCD

Baer, Lee. *Overcoming Your Obsessions and Compulsions.* New York: Plume/Penguin Books, 1992.

Chansky, Tamar E. *Freeing Your Child from Obsessive-Compulsive Disorder.* New York: Three Rivers Press, 2000.

Ciarrocchi, Joseph W. *The Doubting Disease: Help for Scrupulosity and Religious Compulsions.* New York: Paulist Press, 1995.

Foa, Edna B., and Reid Wilson. *Stop Obsessing!: How to Overcome Your Obsessions and Compulsions.* New York: Bantam Books, 1991.

Jenike, Michael A., Lee Baer, and William E. Minichiello. *Obsessive-Compulsive Disorders: Practical Management.* 3rd ed. St. Louis, MO: Mosby-Year Book, 1998.

Osborn, Ian. *Tormenting Thoughts and Secret Rituals.* New York: Dell, 1998.

Penzel, Fred. *Obsessive-Compulsive Disorders: A Complete Guide to Getting Well and Staying Well.* New York: Oxford University Press, 2000.

Schwartz, Jeffrey M. *Brain Lock.* New York: Regan Books, HarperCollins, 1996.